D1080119

The Mistress

The Mistress

The Mistress

Wendy James
and
Susan Jane Kedgley

Abelard-Schuman · London

©1973 Wendy James and Susan Jane Kedgley
First published 1973
ISBN 0 200 72102 X

Abelard-Schuman Limited
450 Edgware Road   24 Market Square
London W2   Aylesbury Bucks

Printed in Great Britain by Willmer Brothers Limited,
Birkenhead

Contents

Acknowledgments

Extracts and references in *The Mistress*:

Alex Comfort, *Sex in Society*, Duckworth
Elliott Roosevelt, *An Untold Story: The Roosevelts of Hyde Park*, Putnam's, New York
A. J. P. Taylor, *Lloyd George: A Diary By Frances Stevenson*, Hutchinson
Arianna Stassinopoulis, *The Female Woman*, Davis-Poynter
Germaine Greer, *The Female Eunuch*, MacGibbon & Kee
Norman and Jeanne MacKenzie, *The Time Traveller: The Life of H. G. Wells*, Weidenfeld
Erich Fromm, *The Art of Loving*, Allen & Unwin

1 The Mistress - Who is She?

The modern mistress, and the mistress from the past, is the most misjudged of women. She's misjudged because she's misunderstood. No one really knows who she is. Certainly she is never thought of as the ordinary woman down the road who joins in the crush on the underground every morning and shops with everyone else in the supermarket at weekends. Yet this is the reality of the mistress.

Most people, when thinking of the mistress, see her as a fantasized figure from the past, a glamorous figure who added spice to leaden historical periods. She is the Pompadour who ruled a king, she is Emma Hamilton who bewitched a sea lord, she is Eva Braun who comforted a maniac attempting to take over the world, she is the Dark Lady of Shakespeare's life, she is Lady Caroline Lamb who was a muse to a famous poet, she is Missy LeHand, the faithful devoted aide to President Roosevelt.

The mistress is the stuff historical films are made of. She is a fascination and preoccupation of painters, poets, dramatists and writers. She is the most fantasized lady of them all. And fantasy cannot give the true picture.

Because one figure has been taken out of a certain period and has been distorted and exaggerated, it is somehow assumed that this is the way life was for the hundreds of ordinary mistresses of that time. Their lives would have been reflections of the prototype. In fact the reverse is more likely to be closer to the truth. Emma Hamilton's life, despite certain dramatic overtones, was most probably very like the lives of the forgotten mistresses—

humdrum, unromantic, alternating between ecstasy and despair.

Reality and fantasy are so confused that the mistress remains misjudged and misunderstood.

The purpose of this book is to look at the everyday reality involved in being a modern mistress. By doing so we become the apologists for the mistress, past and present. She is an integral part of our society yet must not be considered so. People may despise her existence but we feel that her role is very necessary.

A mistress by our definition is a woman with whom a married man has a parallel relationship, or a woman who, outside her own marriage, has a relationship with another man. All these illicit relationships – i.e. based on adultery – must be long-term and as a yardstick we chose one year as the minimum period of involvement.

The mistress is no longer necessarily 'kept'. In fact the mistress who is lavished upon is the exception today. We came across only one who was and she answered our questionnaire. But we did hear of several, one of whom sounded marvellous – mistress to an MP for ten years, she is alleged to receive £10,000 a year through the liaison. Another – and she is part of our sample of thirty-five mistresses – said she received some money over the years and now that the relationship has ended she receives £500 a year. This she calls her alimony.

More common is the mistress whose gifts from her lover extend to no more than the occasional bottle of wine or a couple of good meals a week. Infrequently a man will help out with the rent on a flat. But most mistresses would refuse this financial assistance because it makes more blatant the reality they try to avoid facing up to – that they *are* mistresses. To all the women in our sample, and even seven of the ten men, this was a derogatory label.

Most of the mistresses we questioned didn't realize that

their descriptions of their roles faithfully followed the definition of a mistress. If they did realize it, they preferred to avoid accepting the reality. This was because they had allowed the confused and stigmatized notion of the mistress to influence their own opinion of themselves.

The mistress is inescapably affected by society's interpretation of her as a woman committing a crime. She finds herself in a paradoxical situation. She is in love – a condition which she has believed from childhood to be the ultimate in womanly fulfilment. Yet because she loves a married man, the achievement of this idealized state is suddenly interpreted as a crime.

She is unable to reconcile her own feelings and the public assumption that what she is doing must be wrong. Instead of realizing that she is a victim of a social situation, she remains confused and bewildered.

She is in a quandary. Should she be a martyr and suppress her powerful feelings in the name of public morality, or should she be true to herself and express her feelings, thereby defying public morality and invoking censure?

It is an invidious position. Whichever road she chooses will probably bring suffering and anguish. It is made worse by the fact that, unlike the suburban housewife or the 'wronged wife', she has not the assistance of the guilt-ridding liberation slogan 'It's not my fault'.

The housewife can blame the breakdown of her marriage on forces beyond her control – her isolation, her child-rearing role, lack of stimulation, her husband's infidelity. She sees herself as the victim of circumstances, whereas the mistress, just as much a victim, has not been allowed to see herself in this way. She has no externals to blame, so all the blame and guilt is turned in on herself.

Few, we found, ever really come to terms with the mistress dilemma – hence the prevalence of masochism among mistresses. The masochist is torn by her own self-guilt and by the guilt of others – a painful situation to be in. But many believe that this pain is the price they must pay for having an illicit love relationship.

A free agent who has managed to rationalize intellectually the problem, and who is therefore able to blame society rather than herself for her castigated social position, is still rare. The masochist who misunderstands her own position and suffers because of it, is still the norm.

Censure occurs even though we are living in a permissive age. While one would have expected 'permissiveness' to extend from the pre-marital scene to the extra-marital scene, this is not the case. Perhaps, with the advent of group sex and husband- and wife-swapping, we are seeing the start of the change. At the same time these are tolerated only when both partners are involved, and this is clearly not the case with the mistress.

The call-girl scandal which involved Lord Lambton and Lord Jellicoe, and the Profumo case before it, have helped to confuse the public about what a mistress is. Newspaper articles at the time proposed that mistresses are prostitutes, but while it is so that a prostitute may become a mistress, a mistress is not a prostitute. She never can be because she is emotionally involved.

Prostitution, group sex and husband- and wife-swapping assume sexual infidelity only, and this is the over-riding difference which distinguishes them from the mistress–lover situation.

A mistress relationship assumes an emotional relationship with all its concomitant involvement, responsibilities, feelings of guilt and dissembling. If it were only sex a man were looking for he would presumably choose the earlier option of prostitution. This is indeed one of the speculated reasons why Lord Lambton chose call-girls when a man with his money, good looks, personality and intel-

10

ligence could probably have had just one woman out-side his marriage. If he had had a mistress he would have been less open to blackmail.

However, if he had announced to the world that he had had a mistress rather than liaisons with call-girls, the public reaction would have been very different. Super-ficial relationships, such as one-night stands, are tolerated whereas deeper, more meaningful relationships are much more feared. Even the most *avant-garde* (proponents of group sex included) would shy away from the idea of a mistress. There is a world of difference between emotional and sexual infidelity.

Advocates of wife-swapping etc. use as their defence the fact that a marriage is more liable to be sustained if this sort of 'variety' is indulged in. Prostitutes are toler-ated for the same reason. As Alex Comfort observed in *Sex in Society*: 'Men who have no moral or aesthetic objections to intercourse with prostitutes figure less often in the divorce courts than those who have, because their lapses are usually undetected; it is probably the more sensitive types who cannot accept a wholly physical esti-mate of coitus who get into the most trouble, by incurring new responsibilities and by establishing a positive emotional relationship with their mistresses.'

In other words the prostitute is seen as a marriage-maker, a mistress as a marriage-breaker. While we found that many mistresses do perform a marriage-making function, the fact that this aspect of their role is so seldom recognized has meant that having a mistress is seen as the most taboo of all extra-marital activities.

The word mistress has no masculine equivalent. Throughout history a woman with a lover or lovers has been given a whole range of derogatory labels — whore, harlot, prostitute, fallen woman, scarlet woman. The man is described only as a lover, a word devoid of all critical moral judgment.

11

The mistress-lover situation, as we will elaborate, is predicated upon the double standard. The man *has* a mistress. She exists only in relation to him – e.g. Lord Nelson is never described as Emma's lover. Indeed implicit in the word mistress is that she has a master, that she is the possession of a male.

Though she is no longer financially owned, as was the Victorian kept woman, we found that most men attempt emotional possession. While accepting their right to be unfaithful, they simultaneously demand total fidelity on the part of their mistresses – and most mistresses accept this double standard as well.

The mistress has been assumed to exist to satisfy the sexual and emotional needs of her lover. Few have ever considered that a mistress had sexual and emotional needs of her own. In a classic dominant-subordinate relationship, she was there to be used by him, although a few like Lady Conyngham (mistress to George IV of England), Lola Montez (mistress to Ludwig I, King of Bavaria) and Madame Pompadour (mistress to Louis XV of France) certainly learnt how to turn the situation to their own advantage.

These women were outstanding and today would probably be influential in their own right, while a modern ambitious woman would probably be more concerned about using a man to her own advantage.

In fact the changing social and economic role of the female has made a considerable difference to the mistress just as it has to other women. It means that instead of sitting around waiting for a man to notice her, the present-day financially independent mistress *can* choose and use. Unlike the mistress of the past, who depended totally on her master for food and income, the modern-day mistress does not have such intense feelings of obligation. She is not at the mercy of the will and whim of her lover.

It is now possible for the mistress to have a life of her own, even alternative lovers. Because she has a career and ambition, she will be less likely totally to revolve round her lover. And in having this outlook and the advantages that come from it, she will be better off than most wives.

For the first time independent-minded women are seeing that there are definite advantages in being a mistress. This type of mistress is indeed revolutionary. She is the antithesis of her Victorian counterpart.

When we set out to find mistresses to interview, friends and acquaintances assured us it would be an almost impossible task. Most of them thought they were few and far between and were certain that they were mistresses only if they were kept.

But when we spread the word that we were looking for them, we were astonished by the numbers we found. Not all of them would answer our questionnaire but we had no difficulty in finding our sample. (It must here be stressed that this was never intended to be a scientific sample – the book is rather an interpretation of the answers given by a selection of thirty-five women.)

Our preconceptions about the mistress as a glamorous, young, single woman were rapidly shattered as we found ourselves talking to an extremely varied cross-section of female society.

We found that the norm is still the single woman, and a fairly attractive single woman at that. But also in our sample are women who could be described only as plain, nervous, withdrawn, shy. In fact from the range of personality types it was impossible to generalize.

All the interviews were done in Britain but the countries of origin were: Britain, United States, Australia, New Zealand, Holland, Eire and Germany.

What they all had in common was that they were all middle-class. All but two were involved in some professional occupation, though eleven originally came from working-class backgrounds. They were to be found in journalism, publishing, university and medical work, or in allied areas such as secretarial work and public service. Three were housewives, two without outside work interest.

The ages of the women ranged from twenty-two to fifty-five: thirteen were between twenty-two and thirty, sixteen between thirty and forty, five between forty and fifty, and one above fifty. Two mistresses had children by their lovers.

For reasons of time and economics, the modern mistress is a middle-class 'luxury' object. For a man to have a mistress he must have unaccountable time and money as well as energy and freedom from guilt. If he shares a joint banking account with his wife and has a rigid nine-to-five work routine, he's not in the running.

The man best situated to have a mistress, according to one of our well-seasoned male lovers, is a wealthy businessman working erratic hours, married to a woman preoccupied with children and who has grown to accept her husband's prolonged 'business trips'. We interviewed ten men and all were financially well off, all had work reasons to be able to be away from home constantly; nine had children.

Personality characteristics were again wide-ranging; as to their looks, six of the ten looked quite ordinary, two could be described as handsome, two as attractive. The jobs our men were involved in were: journalism, publishing, rag trade, broadcasting, advertising, university and legal (all occupations where there is considerable opportunity for them to meet single or available women). The men's ages ranged between early thirties and late forties. Of the forty-five men and women interviewed, thirty-three had met their mistresses or masters at work, or in some related activity – for example, a social function.

The late twenties and early thirties was the age group in which we found women had become mistresses almost from necessity. Single men held no attraction for them. Two of the men in their late forties mentioned that they had become involved because of a 'now-or-never feeling' as their fiftieth birthdays loomed ahead. The other main reason compelling men to look, consciously or unconsciously, for mistresses was failings in their own marriages (chapter 13, 'The Mistress – The Symbol of the Failure of Monogamy').

The most dramatic variation occurred in the lengths of the involvements. One affair had lasted for twenty-seven years, six had lasted for seven to ten years, five for six years, and the rest between one and four years. In fact three of the long-term affairs had been going for as long as the parallel marriages had. Given that most of the lovers' meetings took place two or three times a week on average (as well as at work in some cases) it is obvious the affairs were very deep. They were not passing fancies and clearly filled a need, for in hourly terms most of our sample spent as much time with their mistresses each week as they did with their wives.

Some relationships had evolved into marriage without title, always with the difference that they were devoid of the stresses and social acceptance of recognized marriages.

Most of the relationships developed in a rather cloistered world. The mistresses and their lovers lived separate lives with little overlap between them except for the intense moments together.

In a hothouse situation like this feelings of infatuation which drew the lovers together in the beginning could be sustained for a long period of time. When they meet they can concentrate exclusively on each other without interference from the normal encumbrances of a marriage. Such relationships have all the fantasy ingredients – excitements, knife-edged insecurity and secrecy.

We have preserved the anonymity of our sample because there was always a third person involved, either the wife or the husband. Several wanted to stand up and be counted – mistresses, that is – because they saw no reason why they should hide or be embarrassed by their relationships. But in the interest of the other mistresses who felt insecure or self-conscious and awkward in their role, they accepted our decision not to publish names or give clues that might lead to their identity being revealed.

Many mistresses were curious to know whether other mistresses were just like them. Did they have the same anxiety feelings, the same problems? Involved as they were in a secret pursuit, they had no obvious guidelines to follow – after all, who's ever heard of a guide book for mistresses?

There is no typical mistress, just as there is no typical wife. However, it may be said that she does not correspond with the fantasized historical prototypes responsible for her reputation.

Our first concern in writing this book was for mistresses and their lovers. They are involved in difficult and stressful situations and it might help them to know that others are in a similar state. Where can a mistress go with her problems? Only to psychiatrists, because marriage guidance doesn't cater for her, nor can she usually turn to her mother or local vicar for a sympathetic ear. Mostly she turns in on herself.

We found in researching material for this book that there is almost nothing constructive written about her. The historical biographies have little value for the modern mistress. We feel she should be able to see herself in perspective – as a symbol of the failings of monogamy rather than the contemptuous figure she is so frequently portrayed as.

Having ourselves experienced the self-guilt, the anguish, the social disapproval and the aloneness of being a mistress, we realize in retrospect that much of this could have been avoided if we had had the knowledge and insight we gained from writing this book.

2 The Mistress - The Masochist

'I realize now I was never really in love with my lover and I went through a hell of a lot of pain that I now regret. I was a late starter. I was thirty-seven and although I'd had a couple of affairs I'd never been in love. If I'd been a happier person I might have been able to withstand the effects of the relationship I formed. Instead I allowed it all to happen to me by putting aside my true feelings.

'I got to know both him and his wife through work. Of course, because it was his job that brought us into contact, I knew him better than I did her, but I was friendly with her in a superficial sort of way. They had been married eighteen years. I liked him, I liked his personality, but I never imagined there could be anything between us. I was terribly naïve.

'We both went away on the same job. We were away for two weeks and he gave me no peace. He was courting me, and he's just as persuasive as a lover as he is as a writer. I was flattered . . . I think I must have been half alive until that time. When he told me he was deeply in love with me the crime, my crime, started – I was dishonest with myself. I became involved with him, and yet I knew I wasn't in love with him. But I believed he loved me and that was all that mattered at that stage. No man had ever loved me like that before.

'I knew he'd had other affairs during his marriage but this one obviously meant something more. At least, if the wife's reactions were anything to go by it did. She found out about our affair and immediately rang the office and told the boss. Then she sent a private detective to see me asking if I were willing to be named so that she could get an uncontested divorce for adultery.

'Things were really happening too fast. She threw him out and he took a flat. I resigned from my job because I thought it would be the best thing to do to avoid a scandal. At the office nobody wanted me to go but I couldn't think of anything else to do. He was quite hopeless in the flat by himself, completely inept at looking after himself. So I moved in. I became his cook, his cleaning lady, his typist. Even at that stage I don't think he meant to use me.

'We'd hardly had time to establish our relationship but he insisted that he did want to marry me. After a few months he asked his wife when the divorce would be coming through and she said it never would. She wouldn't let him back into the house to see the children and he was very unhappy. I wanted to leave then, to make a break, but he kept telling me that he loved me, that I was his life and he couldn't live without me, and so I stayed. I honestly don't think that a wedding ring was my goal with him and the lack of divorce didn't worry me. We established a fairly happy routine and I advanced his career a great deal. I wrote two books for him, did all his typing, wrote his lectures. In fact I think I earned quite a lot of our money. I was not only a wife by this time, I was also his secretary and the main support of his wife and children in their large country house.

'Then the new divorce laws came in, and to all intents and purposes he could have got his divorce and settled the whole problem. But his wife turned on the emotional blackmail – she was going to have a nervous breakdown, would commit suicide if he got a divorce. She used all the threats she knew would tear him in half. And they did. He obviously promised that he would never divorce her and we now had to face up to a situation that would never be stable and permanent. I did a lot of crying then – night after night I was drained by emotion. I didn't know what to do. I know now that I should have left there and then but instead I decided to stay with the situation. Despite all the heart-rending and the anguish, I was fairly happy.

'There was just one thing about him I couldn't bear – his possessiveness. He never wanted me to have any friends, male or female. Because I was uncertain about my future anyway, I decided to become a freelance journalist which required me to do interviews which I could sell. He didn't like this, he was jealous of the time I wasn't with him and it culminated in him driving me to the interviews and sitting outside in the car. As most of my interviews were with men, he presumed I'd be getting up to something with them. I must admit it was flattering in a way. To have my lover think that I could "get up to something" just like that was quite a boost to my morale.

'I became busier and busier and then my parents were ill and I had to go to them at weekends. He hated this. Our sex became less and less frequent and the strain on me was eventually too much. I completely broke down physically – I was not only working hard for him, for myself, but also for my parents. I lost an awful lot of weight and became quite ugly-looking. I was really at my lowest ebb.

'More than at any other time, I needed his sympathy, his love. Instead I discovered a hotel bill for two in his pocket – when he should have been with me he was with another dolly. When I found this it was as though I'd had an electric shock. I was down and he kicked me – even now, two years later, I feel the same resentment. I'd been trapped into a ludicrous situation by him and his wife. All his pleadings about his love for me meant nothing. Not only had he made love to another woman, I also found out he had been seeing his wife as well. I had been an absolute fool.

'There was no reason to hang around now, to find

reasons for maintaining the relationship. I packed up and took off for six weeks' holiday in America. I eventually came back to London and it took him ten months to find me. It was pathetic the way he tried to persuade me to go back to him. He even tried to convince me he was living with his mother when I knew that he'd gone back to his wife.

'Her resentment played a great part in the misery in our lives together. She wanted to make us as unhappy as possible, not only holding the divorce above our heads for two years, but also calling me a temptress and sorcerer. Nothing could convince her that he was attracted to me. She was very cruel to me. At one time she turned up at the flat and gave me a lecture in front of a friend. What was she trying to do? Her marriage had been bad. They had had row after row, she being as temperamental as he. Before I ever got involved with him she used to moan to me about him and she enjoyed cutting him down to size in front of other people. She had a definite double standard. She decided to accept his two previous affairs, but not me. I was different – perhaps because she saw me as a real threat. She knew that he had reached a certain point as a public figure and her biggest threat was that she would write to the *News of the World* and let everyone know what we were up to.

'I always had a very guilty feeling about her. There was no one to blame in the end but me. I had decided to start the affair and keep it going. I was deceiving her but it would have been someone else if it hadn't been me. I think he took a certain pride in showing me off to her. He wanted to prove something to her – perhaps because she undermined him so much.

'Mistresses today, so far as I'm concerned, are second wives. My lover used to call me his wife and I was faithful and loyal. He didn't believe such things mattered. Although he'd been unfaithful to his wife I felt it was a terrible thing for him to do it to me. He had betrayed me and I made up my mind there and then that the relationship had changed irrevocably.

'I was used, but I was also willing to be used because I did feel a certain love for him. I have even today a great affection for him. I care about him and about what happens to him. I've gone on working with him professionally and, just as I did when I was his lover, I try to boost his ego rather than dampen it.

'Mistress seems such an old-fashioned term. It belongs to the Victorian and Edwardian times when mistresses were set up and had all the good things. I certainly wasn't kept. In fact I helped to keep somebody else – I paid half the rent, worked for my living, for our living. I paid my way.

'I'm sure that if his marriage had been good, I couldn't have become the object of his affection the way I did. You can't steal a loving husband from his wife. And when a marriage is bad people can recognize it. Some of the people we knew were stuffy about our relationship but others, like my parents, were marvellously understanding. In this way society's attitude is changing – if the marriage isn't working, there must be another way.

'I know the relationship I had was masochistic. I'm still recovering from it. A stronger and happier person would have walked out much earlier. It must have been conditioned into me to put up with things that bring pain. It helped me grow up, albeit very late in life. But I also gave up a lot for it. I gave up the job I loved, it changed my life completely. I gave up many of my friends and I suppose that during the four years I was with him he also prevented me meeting a man I might have married. I completely shaped my life around him. I'd never do it again.

'At the moment I'm having an affair with a married man. We both know the score – we have a purely physical

22

relationship. His wife doesn't like sex and we do. We don't ask each other what we've been doing in between our meetings. We both have our freedom, and now I realize just how important that is.'

History has deluded us about the glamour of a mistress's life. Historians try to persuade us that her life was untouched by reality and was filled with endless caviar and unending passion. Nothing could be further from the truth.

For example, one remembers only the sumptuous lifestyle of Emma Hamilton, not the degradation in which she ended her days. One thinks only of the poesy and romance of the relationship between Byron and Lady Caroline Lamb, not the sordid discarding of her when the love had run its course. The beautiful and talented Ada Giachetti Caruso's mistress, should have had it all her own way. But all the champagne and applause in the world could not have compensated her for never becoming the singer's wife.

For the mistress, the reality is more likely to be frustrating, lonely and painful. However much she may be in love with her man, the affair must be illicit — adulterous — and very few women are able to survive the emotional, sexual and social tensions that arise when dishonesty is forced to become a way of life.

'When a mistress goes out with her man she is forced to be incredibly underhand and clandestine. She can't demonstrate her emotions in public because there might be someone around who would recognize him. She's got to be cool and controlled. She's got to be dishonest to herself.'

There is definitely no glamour in sitting by a telephone waiting for it to ring. There is definitely no glamour in the frustration that occurs when the mistress cannot, under any circumstances, ring her lover, because once he has left their meeting place he enters his own world where she would be an intruder.

If her lover has become her whole life and she has discarded friends and other social contacts, she will be continually thinking of ways to kill time, to get her through those expectant hours before she sees her lover again.

She will find herself clenching her teeth and wallowing in self-pity as she watches her lover disappear from her bed. She will yearn for him to stay by her side so that she can experience the pleasure of waking beside him in the morning. Instead she will wake alone with only the ringing of the alarm to remind her that another day has begun. Her lover is most probably giving his good-morning kiss to his wife.

'Ours was a very loving relationship, but I used to get incredibly frustrated when I wanted to talk to him and he wasn't around. I was fortunate that he lived in another city for if I was really desperate I could usually get hold of him. But it was unbelievably complicated – ringing friends who would ring friends. That sort of thing. During weekends there was absolutely no way of getting hold of him so I used to go away a lot, just to give myself something to do, to get him off my mind.'

Because it is a partial, part-time relationship the mistress will have to cancel engagements, to put off making dates in advance – just in case her lover might want to see her that night. If she is not available, who knows when he will be free again?

The more a mistress shapes her life around her absentee lover, the less she takes herself and her feelings into account. Often she will subjugate herself completely,

24

accepting the boy scouts' motto 'Be Prepared' without question.

As the relationship develops she learns gradually that she must live on a diet of snatched moments and subsequent stresses. For all her giving, this is hardly a reward.

'The more deeply involved the mistress is and the more dependent she is on her lover, the more likely she is to get hurt. All the stresses of the situation – your own guilt, feelings of resentment, the imperative constant secrecy, your need of him when you can't have him – all these stresses are compounded as the relationship gets deeper. It gets gradually worse, not better.'

Unlike wives and girlfriends, the mistress does not have someone to show off to her friends and family, though they are very likely to be aware, by her continual refusals to invitations and by her weak excuses, that something is going on. The mistress does not have someone to give her social acceptibility and security.

If she's feeling lonely or ill, she cannot rely on her lover being there to comfort her, to look after her. It's no wonder that many go through periods of depression and psychological breakdown, even make suicide attempts. For women like these, denied the natural responses of a relationship that society smiles on, being a mistress is distinctly an unrewarding, masochistic affair.

The implication of such an attitude is that these mistresses want to be hurt. They are acquiescing in a situation that is painful.

'When we first started the affair, I was a "great personality" – I used to leap around at parties and laugh and sing. I was the real extrovert. My lover wanted me to be "quietly dignified", which meant passive and with-

drawn. He imposed this personality on me. He changed me into a quiet, restricted little lady and wouldn't let me have any life of my own apart from him.

'I remember once going through agonies trying to sneak out to go to a party. For him it was all or nothing. He had to totally possess me, even though I was only his mistress.'

What a mistress expects of the relationship considerably affects her chances of happiness within it. If she is pursuing marriage and ultimate permanency, she is likely to be disappointed. But, being masochistic, she will sometimes build a fantasy around her wishful thinking, so that in her dreams she will become the second wife.

When things are going badly she has the dream to fall back on. When they seem slightly better, perhaps when her lover seems especially reluctant to leave her, she sees this as hope that he will do something about ending his marriage. She will not recognize that the long journey he faces to his home, or the lying and dissembling he must do when he gets there, has anything to do with his hesitation.

She cannot face up to the reality because to do so would be to burst the frail bubble of fantasy that lessens the stress of the relationship.

Because she has become dependent and fears losing him, the mistress will allow herself to follow the will and whim of her lover. It's only later that she realizes just how much agony and humiliation this entailed.

'If I'd been a stronger and happier person I would have walked out earlier instead of letting myself be used as I did. I effectively became a second wife to him. He had made me believe that he would marry me, so I gave up my job, my friends, my flat. I literally gave up everything for him. I was a fool.'

Unlike the free agent who is in control of her life and can opt in and out of the relationship without damage to her emotions, the masochistic mistress seems to be unable effectively to change the pattern of her existence. Because of this she becomes totally a victim of the stresses of an illicit relationship – and she has no resources to avoid them.

Her only security *is this relationship*, however chaotic and demanding it might be. She is completely unable to accept the concept which Germaine Greer talks about in *The Female Eunuch* – 'insecurity is freedom'. She hasn't confidence in herself, so she absorbs the stress rather than letting it bounce off her.

'Sometimes I create dramas to hurt myself and I get into a terrible state about the whole thing. At various stages I've known I should have brought the relationship to an end. I know there can be no happy ending. I know that eventually I am going to be really hurt, but I can't stop myself.'

The misery of some of the women was accentuated by the possessiveness of their lovers who consciously deprive their mistresses of any existence outside the affair. Even in quite long-standing relationships, up to three years, some mistresses allowed their lovers to dominate them completely in this.

'I was utterly miserable and subjugated during my entire time with him. He was completely possessive of me. I wasn't allowed any friends so I gave them all up. I had to – if I ever went and had a drink with somebody he'd become insanely jealous and insist I was having an affair. Yet I spent so much time sitting around waiting for him to come and see me.

'I can't remember enjoying myself at all. I had no say in

my life, yet in a way I think that was what I wanted, or thought I needed. I had never had any discipline in my life and I wanted his authority.

'*When I did recognize just how much it was hurting me, there came a point where I couldn't take it any more. I just couldn't stand being suffocated any longer, so I packed my bags and took off to the other side of the world.*'

Most, of course, don't run away. Five mistresses recognized the masochism in their behaviour yet felt they were unable to do anything about it.

Even in cases where the lover was unfaithful while demanding her fidelity, the mistress found a way to rationalize it. She saw herself as a victim of hopeless passion. This enabled her to blame the situation for every failure and disappointment when clearly some of these failures were aggravated by her own attitude.

The guilt a mistress feels contributes to the masochism. She accepts that what she is doing is wrong in the eyes of society. She judges herself harshly, believing that she is a sinner, someone who deserves contempt. She has no self-esteem and cannot believe that others can respect her.

As she has cut herself off from her friends, she has no one to turn to, no one to use as a yardstick. The relationship is all she has, and if it starts going wrong, she accepts that the hurt is justified.

'*I feel I know all there is to know about grief. I feel I have really been through grief, and if a close relative such as my mother or sister were to die, I could not feel greater grief than that which I experienced. I was like a person crippled in some way. I saw him as my disability.*'

Undoubtedly the most galling aspect of all for the mistress who has become deeply attached to her lover is

28

the knowledge that she must share – physically and emotionally – the man she loves. The symbiotic and exclusive nature of the love she has been conditioned to desire (and to demand) makes the sharing of a lover, and the acceptance of second place in a triangular relationship, particularly chafing.

It means that a mistress must reconcile herself to a life made up of constant giving and self-sacrifice to a man she is in love with. And in return she will receive only partial affection, only partial commitment, partial loyalty and part-time presence.

'I know the priorities in his life are, in this order: his work, his child who he loves and in whom he sees himself immortalized, his wife, then me. I'm not stupid enough to think he would ever leave his wife and child, but when he does talk about going away on holiday with his wife I do feel ugly, miserable and resentful. He knows I'm after a committed relationship and when he thinks I'm getting too involved he deliberately cools it. When I went into the affair I knew I'd get hurt, and I did. I still am being hurt, but I'm still involved.'

Those who cannot come to terms with a subordinate position desperately try to drive a wedge between the man and his wife. By this they hope to secure the love object exclusively for themselves. In a melodramatic way the wife becomes, in their minds, the villain and the persecutor. This exaggeration helps the mistress to convince herself – and to try to convince him – that he would be better off without her.

But the sad irony is that the more frustrated the mistress becomes, and the more demanding and irritable she is, the more likely it is that she will drive her lover away. In effect she will turn herself into a nagging wife, and a man who seeks to avoid this pressure in his own marriage certainly does not want to see it re-created in his relationship with his mistress.

'Because of the intensity of our involvement it was incredibly difficult for me to accept the limitations of the relationship, the possibility that it might end at any time. The deeper the relationship becomes the more time you want to spend with the man and the harder it is not seeing him for long periods of time. These frustrations place new stresses on the whole affair. It becomes a vicious circle.'

Some men, as one disillusioned mistress explained, simply disappear as soon as any pressure or conflict arises. After all, he already has one set of responsibilities in which conflict is inbuilt. He doesn't want another lot.

If the mistress doesn't learn by this experience of being hurt, she is likely to become involved again with a man whose power over her is almost the same. As two mistresses said, 'It's when you're feeling at your lowest that you're at your most vulnerable.'

'I had the normal doubts when I found out he was married – you know, not again; playing second fiddle, never phoning at weekends, when I'm low not being able to get hold of him. But I was having a lean time and I was at my lowest point.'

3 The Mistress - The Free Agent

'Until I became involved with my present lover, I had always revolved my life around men. But this time, right at the beginning, I started to get interested in the Women's Liberation Movement. I was able to use my lover as a guinea-pig in a sense.

'I took things to extremes. I wouldn't go near the kitchen when he was around, or wait for him if he turned up late. Initially this caused quite a bit of conflict because his previous women had been sort of substitute wives who ran around him, cooked for him any hour of the day or night, and generally waited on him hand and foot. They were sexy lap dogs and they had no lives of their own except what he offered them.

'Naturally he had grown to expect this treatment as a lover's prerogative. He would turn up at two in the morning and ask for mushrooms on toast. When he'd eaten he'd just sit there waiting for me to jump up and wash the dishes.

'When I explained that I just wasn't going to put up with it, he was shocked at first, but after that I think it was the thing that fascinated him more than anything else. He became intrigued by the life I led. The more independent I became the more clinging he became.

'He told me the second time we met that he was married. I didn't mind at all. I didn't want to marry him so it didn't matter. If I had wanted to marry him I suppose I would have cared but this way there was no struggling with guilt or wrestling with a conscience. I knew that if it wasn't me it would be someone else.

'I've never believed a mistress can break up a happy

marriage. His wasn't good then but I think it's a little better now just because he's having a good time sexually and intellectually. He always felt deprived in these areas in his marriage but now he goes home a happier person and therefore a better husband.

'In some ways it has been a godsend that he is married. In fact I think it was the saving grace of our relationship, because he hasn't been able to put many of the pressures on me that otherwise he might have. He would have wanted to move in with me. I would have refused and he would have seen this refusal as a sign of rejection. Because he has accepted the fact that I don't want to marry him or live with him, our relationship has survived.

'I see as much of him as I want and there are times when I am pleased to tell him to go back to his wife and family. At one stage, when he was talking about how neurotic his daughter was becoming, I insisted he spend more time at home.

'But I don't want to know about his wife and kids. They don't feature in my life or get in the way of our relationship. I never hear him say, "I've got to get home to the wife." Perhaps if I did I might resent her, but in fact she never impinges on us at all. I'm only interested in her as an objective study of what happens to women housebound in a marriage, and to that extent I feel sorry for her.

'My lover has told me that she is the product of a strict Catholic upbringing. She wouldn't use contraceptives and so she got kids she didn't want and became permanently tied to the house. She's lost all confidence in herself. Before her marriage she showed promise as an actress and she could obviously try and start again, but she can't leave the security of the home even to audition.

'I don't think she knows about me because her husband often has to work through the night in his job. She is used to the routine of him being out five nights a week. In some ways I suspect she is relieved he is away so much. He says she never makes any fuss about it.

'I know I am a symptom of failure in his marriage, every sort of failure. For both of them it seems a disastrous marriage. He didn't want children in the first place so now he doesn't like them. He longs to have a child he has planned. The sex between him and his wife is non-existent because she is afraid of becoming pregnant again. They have no mental communication at all. He's had hundreds of girlfriends through the years. He wants to leave her and I am sure he will when he can afford it financially.

'I've had two experiences with married men before this. The first was my first sexual experience and it was quite important to me. Both affairs lasted about six months and I learnt a lot about sex. They were older than I was, were very good teachers and not fumbling amateurs – which is what a young woman needs when she wants to find out what it's all about.

'The relationship with my present lover has been going for nearly eighteen months and it has been really important to me. I have learnt a lot through it. I have learnt that relationships with men are much better if a woman retains her own life, her own interests and individuality. I'd never done that before.

'I can't see the relationship going on much longer, however. We're both ready for a change and when the time comes there won't be any recriminations, heartsearching and guilt. It will end cleanly because we've been honest with each other right the way through and neither has been possessive or demanding of the other.

'At the moment I'm too much in the process of growth to even consider getting married. I imagine I will want to some day when I'm more ready for it. I have definite career plans and I would never consider giving them up to take up a career as housewife.

'I am going to be financially independent whether I marry or not. I certainly would not live off a husband. My idea of marriage isn't the conventional orange-blossom idea – to me it just means living with somebody more or less permanently and sharing something with him. Not now though. I'm not prepared to take the risk until I'm a fully developed person.'

In our interviews we found half a dozen women who, in sharp contrast to the masochist, seemed thoroughly to enjoy being a mistress. They are not predators – i.e. women intent on sleeping their way to the top. They are simply women, four of them in their late twenties, two in their early thirties, who relish the freedom and independence that are part of the right mistress–lover relationship.

We have called this type of mistress the free agent because, like the hetaera, the courtesan in Ancient Greece, she is never subordinated or possessed. Far from existing solely to give her lover pleasure, as did the Victorian kept woman, today's free agent sees her independence as the cornerstone of her relationships.

Our society has yet to recognize any mistress role as legitimate and desirable, but the Grecian courtesan was accepted as a respectable marriage parallel. She had her own children, her own way of life. The woman who was bred to be a courtesan could not be happy in the conventional restricted life-style of the Grecian wife. She was able to select her lovers and remain stimulating to them in a way that was beyond the average captive wife.

There was no need for the courtesan to hide herself away. She could take her place in public without fear of scorn or derision. And because she had the freedom to grow and develop as an individual she was, it was widely accepted, a more interesting, influential and intelligent woman than the average wife.

Today's free agents, we found, see their independence, lack of deep commitment and partial attachment as positive assets.

'I prefer to be a mistress. I wouldn't marry my lover even if he left his wife. I prefer being the other woman – it's a more exciting caviar relationship. You're not taken for granted as you are when you become a wife.'

Just as the woman in our case history does, free agents believe that the secret of their success lies in having lives of their own. All six were either committed to their present roles or to furthering a definite career.

They have their own friends, their own interests, their own ambitions, and they are not prepared to put aside any of these for their lovers, indeed any man. They are also adept in keeping their two worlds separate.

The four who are not married are career women – yesterday's spinsters and 'blue-stockings' have become today's swinging single girls. They are self-confident and assertive. All free agents recognize a need for expressing their sensuality and realize because of their independent frame of mind that they do not want a society-approved courtship which eventually leads to marriage. In their terms their reasons for choosing their sexual partners are valid.

'The single men I meet in the normal course of a day are either homosexual, mother's boys or insecure men who are quite unable to cope with me. Being mistress to a married man is the only alternative I have to being a hermit.'

Because free agents do not have the same goals as the

more traditional young woman they deliberately avoid situations where they are forced to be influenced about their futures.

'In most relationships with single men there comes a time when you either go off and live together or you stop seeing each other. These sorts of pressures are absent when you're going out with a married man. You can just go out with him and enjoy it – and you don't have to think of the future all the time.'

The difference between the free agent and other mistresses is her strong personality, her self-confidence. She doesn't require the same degree of security and reassurance. In fact she comes close to being what American psychologist Abraham Maslow called 'a self-actualized individual'. After a close study of such people, Maslow found that self-actualizers are flexible, spontaneous, simple and natural. They have a strong commitment to life and are seen to enjoy it. They appear independent, accept and enjoy solitude and tend to have a philosophical sense of humour. They can enjoy sex far beyond the possibility of the average person even though it doesn't play a central role in their philosophy of life. They are sexually honest and uninhibited and do not need to be aggressive towards the other sex.

Self-actualizers do not make a great distinction between the sexes and do not see the male as essentially the active partner and the female the passive. They can play both roles as occasion and whim demand.

So, like the 'self-actualized individual', the free agent does not become dependent on her lover and could even avoid a really intense involvement.

Men, to her, are not potential husbands. Usually she has either made a conscious decision not to get married (our two married free agents do not, of course, fit in with this – they were already married when they started to realize their goals were different) or to postpone marriage until she feels she is ready for it. Usually she is not satisfied that she is fully developed as a person, and in getting to know herself better she feels she will have more to offer the man she eventually marries. In the meantime she is not above using men for her own purposes.

'I knew I wanted to concentrate on my career but as my work is mainly with other women, I needed a man to give me warmth and love, to remind me of my femininity. A single man might not have accepted the restrictions of such an arrangement. My married lover did.'

A free agent's attitude is pragmatic rather than starry-eyed. She weighs up the advantages, works out whether the relationship will increase or curtail her freedom, whether it will give her pleasure and enjoyment without too much stress. In her awareness of the dangers inherent in a stress situation, the free agent is the antithesis of the masochist. The free agent will avoid stress, the masochist accepts it.

In short, the free agent enters a relationship with her eyes open, and she'll be fully aware of the consequences of her actions. She will use the situation to her advantage.

As her freedom is of ultimate importance, she won't involve herself in domesticity and everyday routine for her lover. She won't be waiting up for him with a meal already prepared, she would not sew on a button for him or wash his shirt. She has no wish to be a wife and she wants to show her lover that there is a difference between her as his mistress and the woman he calls his wife.

'A danger many women don't see is that they tend to become like his second wife. You mustn't do that or you

will eventually smother him. I went through the stage of
just sitting around waiting for a man, getting miserable
and making him feel terribly responsible. You become just
like a second wife, a real burden that he will come to
resent.'

Because she is adamant about not involving herself in mundaneness, the free agent is wined and dined in style. She uses her time well, and is able to devote some of it to the glamour and tinsel of the relationship. As her lover will see her only by pre-arrangement and is not likely to arrive unannounced, she will have had as much time as she needs to prepare herself for him. She will concentrate on her lover and on making herself pleasing to him.

But inbuilt in her is an unpredictability, and because of it her lover can never take her for granted. She of all mistresses is able to play up the mystery element, to give or not give information about herself as she chooses. This puts her in an enviable position where sex is concerned. She knows that her lovers will come to her bed out of desire, not from duty or obligation.

As Germaine Greer wrote in *The Female Eunuch*: 'Lovers who are free to change remain interesting. A lover who comes to your bed of his own accord is more likely to sleep with his arms around you than a lover who has nowhere else to sleep.'

Sex is a major consideration for the free agent. In fact we found that she will let the relationship continue only if the sexual side develops as well. Previous affairs have made her aware of her sensuality and this has encouraged her to want more. A free agent inclines towards older men because she feels they will be more experienced lovers.

'I was twenty-one and he was ten years older. At first he

was teacher and I was his pupil, but after a while our interest in sex developed at the same pace. I'd slept with one man before him, a man about my age, and there was no comparison. He had no understanding of me and my feelings.'

Experimentation is considered natural, for a free agent desires to have the full range of her emotions brought out.

'He wants to go through the book and that's OK with me. He asks me to do things he'd never ask his wife to do – like troilism or group sex. He is really grateful that I agree to these things. If he's a dirty old man then I'm a dirty old woman because I enjoy it too. He's proud of my ability in bed and he wants to show me off by having others there. With me he can have fantasies he can bring into the relationship.

'We use each other in a kind of partnership. He's terribly concerned about whether he does satisfy me and takes a great deal of trouble to make sure he does.'

Two married mistresses we talked to accepted that they fitted our definition of a free agent. They felt that outside relationships made them better at their jobs of being wives and mothers. Both had become involved in an affair after about four years of marriage, and in both cases the liaison has been long-term. (The 1953 Kinsey Report showed that 10 per cent of the women interviewed had carried on extra-marital affairs that had lasted over ten years.)

'I have a lover for sexual reasons only. Sex in my marriage became like one of the chores, like doing the dishes. I was a very staid person but I discovered how different I was when someone paid me special attention.

*My lover and I agreed that we wouldn't fall in love or try
and run off with each other or anything like that.*

'*We both have too many responsibilities so we agreed
to make it just a sexual thing and it's been a great success.
The relationship's been very good for me; it's taught me I
can do all sorts of things with my life. I've blossomed so
much that my husband keeps asking me if I'm having an
affair. I can even deny it without feeling guilty because
I'm not a threat to anybody's marriage. Being a mistress is
a terrific ego trip, much better than a trip to the
hairdresser's.*'

While the single mistress is more likely to meet her
lover in the evenings, the married mistress is forced to
meet him in the glamourless light of day. But this is not
seen as important – because neither misunderstands the
other's attitude to the involvement; the relationship is
stable.

'*There are advantages in us both being married. And
it's in both our interests to stay married to our present
spouses. He's never talked about leaving his wife nor I
about leaving my husband. In fact we'd never contem-
plate any discussion like that.*'

In just one area the married mistress is vulnerable – she
will often have to seek the help of a friend in order to
meet the commitments of the affair. Someone will have to
collect the children after school, do the shopping, even
cover the mistress's traces with a lie when necessary. It
takes a lot of courage to put yourself in the hands of a wife
who could disapprove of the role.

'*I came close to disaster once when a neighbour I
thought my friend took a dislike to my having this*

freedom. I used to pay her to pick up the children and look after them for a couple of hours till I got back. I think she thought the money came from my lover because she suddenly started spreading rumours about me which implied I was a prostitute. Luckily none of these rumours ever got to my husband but I kept right away from her after that.'

Things don't always go right for the single free agent either. Her lover can become dependent, can misjudge her feelings or at least can believe that below the facade deep feelings are just waiting to be set free. This is one of the stresses she can hardly prepare herself for.

'Unfortunately he thinks he's in love with me which makes it rather awkward. He moved into my flat while I was away – left his wife and moved in. This was something I'd never bargained for. At times I feel quite resentful at having my independence taken from me like this. I'm just not ready for a permanent or exclusive relationship.'

The mistress in this situation has allowed her lover to dominate her. By allowing him to stay with her she has temporarily lost her freedom but she now must prove that she can stand on her own two feet, even if necessary using them to push him out of her life. The unwritten rule of the free agent is that she considers herself first.

Obviously the free agent is in an exceptional position. From our discussions with them and with others, she is still the exception, not the rule. Out of the thirty-five mistresses interviewed, the free agents were the only ones thoroughly reconciled to their roles and the only ones who continually derived great pleasure from their affairs.

Previous less satisfactory, even traumatic, encounters with married men had taught them a lot. They had learnt

41

not to expect too much, and they had certainly learnt not to let their lovers expect too much from them.

By not shaping their lives around their lovers, they don't become inextricably involved. They are sceptical rather than naïve, and are self-interested rather than masochistic. They are determined to remain as independent as possible, and to avoid a situation that might lead them to collapse into dependence and submissiveness.

'For seven years our relationship was great. We saw each other about four nights a week, and for two months every year when his wife went upstate to their summer home I moved in with him. The situation could have gone on for ever but I found I had reached a stage in my career where further experience was necessary. I was offered a job in Britain and decided to take it. Only after I'd crossed the Atlantic did I realize that by thinking only about myself and my career I had brought the relationship to an end.'

The free agent concentrates on developing attitudes that are necessary for her to enjoy being a mistress. We encountered two long-term relationships (one of six years, another of three) in which the woman had not become too deeply involved with her lover and was able to have other relationships as well, almost equally long-standing. These women were dedicated mistresses with no interest at present in marriage.

Only in one area is the free agent as susceptible as any other mistress – when the affair escalates into deep involvement on her own as well as her lover's part. Several mistresses who had started off with rational independent attitudes, had gradually found themselves succumbing to irrational behaviour and expectations as their emotional involvement intensified.

Despite their intellectual commitment to independence

42

and personal responsibility, they found themselves wanting to be dependent and possessed. It takes an unusual woman to win against those feelings, so perhaps it will take a long time to bring about an increase in the number of free agents. They are rare, but they are the most 'together' of all the mistresses.

4 The Mistress - The Sex Object

'He'd been my husband's friend for as long as our marriage. I was used to seeing him around the house, used to him dropping in for meals. I was even used to the friendly hug, the kiss on the cheek that friendship brings. He was living in a relatively happy way with a woman but it was a relationship I didn't appreciate then. It was a non-possessive relationship. They both had freedom to do as they chose – and as she didn't particularly have much in common with us she very rarely visited.

'He and my husband were "the boys" together – Peter Pans in pursuit of the hangover, the experience that would make them laugh, give them new jokes to add to their vast boring repertoire. I must admit that I didn't like either of them very much, especially after the birth of my third child. I had terrible baby blues and the physical effort of looking after three children under five years and a husband on shift-work, depressed me physically as well as mentally.

'I used to drive him to work every day but I got so behind in organizing myself that I'd just throw my duffel coat over my nightie, comb my hair and we were ready to go. I can't remember ever wanting to get out of my nightie. I was so short of sleep all I wanted to do was to be ready to sleep when I could.

'My husband had not been the right lover for me for most of the years of our marriage. He usually had to have been drinking to get an erection. I got quite neurotic about the way he'd arrive home in the middle of the night all beery-breathed. First there'd be the hand that would

44

slide across from the other side of the bed, then it would sort of run up and down my side. If I turned away he'd pull me towards him – never speaking a word. Sometimes he'd kiss me, and often his breath was so awful I'd turn away. He was never really deterred. He'd just press on till he came. I can remember now how much it hurt. He never took time to arouse me so there was no lubricating response from me. He never asked me what I felt.

'He started going away more and more often on jobs – or whatever. At least he wasn't coming home for days on end. I spent most of my time reading when I wasn't with the children and in the library I found as many books on sex and sexual technique that I could. I read them continually, searching for a way to get pleasure. From the descriptions I realized I'd never had an orgasm. I had strange dreams at night about masturbation and on waking I remembered how as a child of fourteen I'd slept with a pillow between my legs and how I'd rubbed up and down against it. I started experimenting but I felt too embarrassed, too guilty to go on. I think in fact I was frightened by the way my body responded.

'One night my husband's friend came round to pick up some do-it-yourself equipment. He brought a bottle of wine with him which we drank while waiting for my husband to arrive from work. When he got there it was after midnight and I offered to drive my husband's friend home. My husband staggered off to bed and we drove off.

'My husband's friend suddenly said, "Why don't you wear make-up like you used to? You used to be very pretty. Now you don't seem to care what you wear." I was very offended. It had nothing to do with him. When we stopped in front of his house, he leant across to kiss me and even though it sounds like fiction, I turned towards him and he kissed me on the nose. We both laughed and

45

then he kissed me properly. I felt something like a chord inside me tighten, a pleasurable tightening that made me want more. He said, "I'll come and see you next Tuesday," and that's the way it began.

'All the words I'd read in books suddenly had meaning. Cunnilingus, fellatio, orgasm. He pulled the settee mattress on to the sitting-room floor in front of the fire and he made love to me so beautifully – I'd never felt so free. I think for the first time I realized what sensuality meant and how much a woman can play a part in intercourse. I was so used to my husband making me believe that it only had full pleasure for men that I was quite shaken by my experience.

'The whole of the next year was fraught with tension and unbelievable joy. My sex-life with my husband satisfied him simply because when the shifting hand made its manoeuvre across the bed, I'd immediately think of his friend and feel wet. Nothing much else changed. Daily, in a domestic sense, I remained a slut. I did not want to look good. I made no attempt to do anything out of the ordinary. Nights were different. When my lover was visiting I made up, dressed up, cleaned the house, even cooked meals for us to have later. Quite often they were never eaten. He was as obsessed by me as I was by him and we preferred to play sex games for as long as we could.

'In company we were as cool as ever, though it took a great deal of control on my part. For the first time in my life I felt coquettish, and wanted to be noticed. I suddenly found other men aware of me too and they paid me compliments, believing that it was motherhood that made me flushed, more congenial.

'Some days I would arrange for a neighbour to have the children and spend the afternoon with him at his flat, but most times he came to my house. Miraculously the children never woke – perhaps it has something to do with a mother's mind concentrating on something else. When we made love I wasn't a mother, or a wife, I was a mistress. I was quite abandoned, and continually surprised myself by my reactions to him.

'He was very good about letting me talk after we'd made love – something I'd never known before. And this was the time we became friends. We laughed together, enjoyed each other. We never talked about my husband for we both had our own relationship with him to cope with. He still had his friendship and drinking bouts with him and this could have gone on for ever. For fourteen months it was magnificent; then the woman he lived with left him. He was quite shattered. Even though my marriage was rocky and unlikely to go on, he didn't see any reason to be the cause of the break-up.

'He decided to emigrate to Australia. We weren't in love – our feelings for each other were based on sex and although we were very close there wasn't much else to keep a relationship going. He was as insecure as I was and we would never have made partners except in bed. I was very sad to see him go, but the legacy he'd left me was an awareness of myself that could never be denied again.

'In those months I had with him I felt I was a mistress. I sought and gave pleasure, which is what I imagine an old-fashioned mistress did. The gain was not in monetary terms, but in realization of self, and that's something money can't buy – unless of course you have intensive psychiatric treatment. And where's the pleasure in that?

'My marriage struggles on, but because of the children only. We both have our freedom now and so really the marriage is unnecessary for any other reason than convenience. He still doesn't understand that sex can be enjoyed equally by a woman. He has what I call a

Victorian outlook which presumes that a woman is there only for a man's pleasure. I think I would welcome him meeting someone who could teach him differently. I can't – he just doesn't turn me on that way.'

The thirty-five mistresses and ten lovers in our sample were unanimous that all their relationships began with a sexual attraction. For all but two sex was a very important ingredient and as the affair developed, it got better and better.

Twenty of the mistresses experienced orgasm for the first time through a relationship with a married man and thirty of the mistresses were interested in learning all they could about sex with their lovers. Most of them said their lovers made them feel uninhibited.

All the men said sex with their mistresses was infinitely better than with their wives. The two women who did not think their sex got better and better put this deterioration down to the fact that through the years of their long relationships (one ten years, the other four years), sex had become 'as boring as any husband's and wife's'.

'For a couple of years sex was passionate. Then a sort of married love developed between us and sex gradually became pleasant and infrequent. Like most marriages, I suppose.'

At the beginning of the relationships, most saw the liaison as something temporary and were surprised that the sexual and other aspects developed as they did. For the majority of men and women in our sample the sexual relationship became far and away the most important and pleasurable in their lives. The women in particular found themselves aroused to an extent never experienced be-

48

fore. The majority put this down to the fact that there was deep emotion as well as sexual attraction involved.

'The whole relationship was rewarding for both of us because it was so beautiful. Every feeling is heightened and one is extended as a person. That's the reward of an affair – though you're often not aware of it at the time.'

The mistress–lover relationship would seem almost to be the ideal for the evolvement of sexuality. The feelings of intensity and infatuation are sustained at high pitch because the lovers often meet exclusively to make love. Time is important too because they can never see enough of each other and going to bed never becomes a ritual.

Passion is able to flourish because a mistress and her lover can maintain an enviable level of fantasy every time they meet.

'It was all fun. We used to pretend we were different people from history. The little flat where we met became the Taj Mahal, the White House, the hot desert, the jungles of Brazil. We played a different game each time and it all revolved around the bed. There was no yesterday and no tomorrow. The world was only that flat.'

Unlike the courtship of a single man and woman which encompasses all sorts of activities, such as meeting friends, relations, going to the cinema etc., before eventually spending the night together, the mistress and lover feel that time is so short they prefer to spend it in bed.

'We never wanted to go anywhere except to our flat. There seemed to be such a short time and so much to say. Any third party would have been intrusive.'

The clandestine quality of the relationship enhances

sexual excitement and anticipation. The secrecy encourages intimacy, and in this atmosphere a mistress and her lover become increasingly uninhibited.

All feelings of obligation are absent – their lovemaking is totally voluntary. Often they will go to extraordinary lengths to be able to make love – dissembling, postponing dates, reorganizing set arrangements, simply because sex is the fuel of the relationship.

Each will go to incredible lengths to increase their potential appeal to the other.

'I found myself making certain my toenails and finger-nails were always clean. I bought all sorts of different coloured underwear—I couldn't go past a shop without going in to see if there was anything new and pretty on the market. I even bought a couple of sexy negligees and threw out my old towelling robe. I wanted to feel glamorous.'

The mistresses talked about spending hours in the bathroom perfuming themselves – making their bodies enticing. The lovers in their turn felt they became more considerate – they were eager to wine and dine their mistresses to create the right atmosphere. A lot of attention was given to foreplay.

While this aspect is often the first thing that disappears from a marriage, in a mistress-lover situation it is essential that it continues if the relationship is to last.

'When his wife found out, we decided we had better be more discreet. We gave up sleeping with one another and instead met once a week in a pub. The whole character of the relationship changed when we stopped making love, and we became just like old friends.'

As the mistress in our case history found, the

mistress-lover relationship is sexually unrestrained and the woman becomes especially enthusiastic because of her awakened sexual drive. But the mistress, like any woman in love, can be amazed at her response.

'I had my first orgasm with him and it came as a shock to me. I was physically incapable of moving during it, and as a woman proud of her independence I felt he'd found a way to dominate me. I was quite resentful of this power until I understood that I had as much power over him when he had an orgasm. After this discovery I was no longer overwhelmed.'

The notion of a mistress existing solely to give her lover pleasure appears to be a thing of the past. It was important to the majority of mistresses interviewed that they were as sexually fulfilled as their lovers.

Far from being a passive object to be used as a man's plaything, the modern mistress is an active, vibrant, sexual partner.

'Our sexual interest in each other was so intense that there were times when we didn't know who was female and who was male. We both felt equal in the dominant role.'

Even when she feels that she's being 'used' in other respects in the relationship, the mistress's sexual interest in her lover will often sustain her.

'Even though I knew I ought to end the whole thing I became obsessed with his body. I dreaded the thought that we would never again make love.'

While for one man sexual relations with his wife

improved both because of guilt and because he was more aroused, five found the reverse. Sex with their wives became an unpalatable duty they felt they had to perform.

'I have an intense sex-life with my mistresses whereas I don't desire my wife sexually at all. I'll knock her off occasionally in the morning if I find I wake up with an erection, but I'm not sexually attracted to her. She's always wanting more sex but normally I get home so late that I'm exhausted. She does complain.'

Because sex can so often be submerged in a marriage between the roles of father, breadwinner, financial wizard and handyman, a man will deliberately seek an affair.

'For a man who is loving by nature and who loves sex, there is only one thing to do: get a mistress where you are the one thing, and one thing only – a lover.'

Once achieving sexual satisfaction away from the marriage, sex within it often seems to become even more difficult and the husband frequently has to fantasize his mistress to get an erection with his wife.

'We only make love every few weeks now. I don't want her to think that I'm frustrated or looking elsewhere for my sex. I don't enjoy making love to her any more. In fact I have to imagine I'm with my mistress to make sex with my wife possible.'

Although sex is a basis for the mistress–lover relationship, especially a long-term affair, emotion gradually develops to provide a warm, loving background. The man and the woman are lovers and nothing more is required of them. In this situation the mistress obviously has a head-start on the wife who has many things to think about. The mistress, without marital and domestic responsibilities, has only to think of the man. And from the man's point of view, for his ego, this is what he needs.

5 The Mistress - The Male Need

'When I look back on my life I realize that I've had an affair for every year I've been alive. I'm fifty now . . . but the affairs of course didn't just last a year. Some were much shorter and there were only really three that I'd call long-term, ones that had major effects on me.

'My present wife, who I married two years ago, was my mistress for twenty-five years. She was, I suppose, the reason for my first marriage breaking up. Once my first wife knew about her, she withdrew from the marriage, so I moved out and in with my mistress. It was ironic, because my first wife used to have affairs and I knew about them. When she knew I was having an affair she went hysterical and drove me away.

'My second-longest relationship lasted twenty years. We were very fond of each other and if the circumstances had been right at the time I might have married her. She was the wife of one of my friends and he left her stranded with three kids. I used to see her at least once a week because she lived near to one of my business interests. I began to support her financially and it grew from that.

'The third affair is major in a different way. And it was an unfortunate experience, because it convinced me that there are a lot of women around who will try and break up a marriage if they think they'll get something out of it. In this case I'd formed the relationship and she was pregnant before I realized what she was about. I'd got involved with her for all the wrong reasons . . . she was a convenience that suited my life at that stage. She went ahead and had the child: it was blackmail of the worst kind. I think I hated her for doing it because I felt it was disgusting to bring a third person into the situation where there could be no love or security. I hated her, I hated myself, I hated everything about the situation. It gave me a fright, I can tell you. I'm now paying a paternity order but it's taught me to be wary. If one woman can do that to you, so can any other.

'My life might not be as it is, and my attitude to women might have been different if I'd had children through either of my marriages. I most probably would have considered myself selfish in having affairs because those could have put the children's futures at risk. Children would have taken the need for affairs away because they require emotional as well as physical energy. I'd have had little left over for anything else.

'As this was not to be, I accepted that I was a person who needed other relationships. I think a prerequisite is being free from guilt – anyone who believes in monogamy and fidelity should not even bother pursuing other women because they won't enjoy them when they get them.

'I never sleep with a woman unless I'm very fond of her and attracted to her: just going to bed with someone I met would be prostitution. Most of my friends, much more traditional than me, rush to the West End clubs when their wives are away and they have free time. They are quite happy to take a hostess or a prostitute to bed just for the night. That sort of thing has never been right for me.

'Most of the women I've had affairs with I've met through my business associations – secretaries, customers, floor ladies. Some women I would see only once a month, others once a week. I've owned several flats through the years, and at one time I shared with another man who had a similar temperament and similar interests in pursuit, so I met my women at these flats or at their own.

'All my affairs have been sexual, though on occasions there's been much more to them than sex. I've always been excessively fond of women and I've always found them much more interesting to be with than men. It's no effort for me to be interested in them as people – but it could be that this is an excuse for my immaturity. I've never felt I've treated women as sexual objects or that I've used them.

'What does a mistress get out of the affair? I think it is up to her. If she is quite aware that I do not intend to marry her, she will enjoy what I will offer her. Perhaps she got involved because she was lonely or because her husband wasn't paying her enough attention and she needed to be taken out more – whatever the reason, I have found that the women I've had affairs with enjoy the extra attention. I've never known an unselfish woman so I expect that at the moment she realizes she's not getting out of the relationship what she wants, she'll throw me over. I'm quite prepared for it always.

'I never expect a woman to be faithful to me. I didn't worry about my first wife's affairs, and if I found out that my second wife was also involved with someone, I'd just say, "Good luck to you." I am truly not possessive in this way. As I know how indulgent I am, it would not be possible for me to have a double standard.

'Just one thing about women disappoints me. All of them – and this cuts across social and intellectual barriers – want in the end to be kept or married. My wife is a very intelligent and a very independent woman, and when it came to the crunch she too wanted to be a wife, to be kept and cared for.

'None of my affairs have been a threat to my present marriage, or even a threat to the relationship I had before we married . . . but they have certainly added spice and incentive to life.

'My present wife is unshockable. She's a very pragmatic lady and she knew very early on in the piece that this is what she wanted. She knew exactly what I was like, and she must have decided that she could put up with it. After all, she could hardly think I was going to be faithful after she had been the reason for my infidelity with my first wife.

'Sometimes she finds out about them – I had to tell her about the paternity order for example, and although she was upset, once she knew that there was no question of me loving her, she accepted it. On other occasions all I've said is, "Sorry, that's the sort of person I am." I have never promised not to do it again or anything like that.

'Time, of course, is a very important factor when you have an attitude like mine. A man who not only can provide his wife with a good standard of living but who also has extensive business interests, is in the best position to have affairs. You must be your own boss, have business that demands your time in the evenings and at weekends. Most women will accept this as an excuse so long as they can reap the financial results. I think I'd have given up long ago if I'd had the mess and complications of a nine-to-five worker. It would be impossible – you have to make excuses not only to your wife but also to your employer. I wouldn't have the capacity to work it out. I'm convinced having affairs is an upper-middle-class (in the economic sense) pleasure : a luxury item in a man's life that few can afford.

'I might be fooling myself but I believe I could have been faithful if I'd been required to. I mean, anybody could put up with one person all his life just as you can put up with all sorts of things. You could put up with living on bread and cheese all your life but you'd miss out on a lot. I believe in living life to the full. I'm well off so I don't see the point of acting half-dead. I've always enjoyed myself and have never believed in the stoical, puritanical tradition. Every so often I wonder whether the women I get involved with, or indeed any woman who has an affair, can get anything satisfactory out of it. A relationship consists more than anything of stolen moments, so why should women bother? I suppose it must partly be the challenge. Few women will ever accept that you can be happily married and yet have affairs.'

A theory long held is that man by nature is not monogamous and this would certainly appear to be the case when a man is affluent, has a lot of freedom and finds that his marriage does not meet all his needs.

The most obvious finding in our forty-five interviews is that most of the lovers were heading for their fortieth birthday or were well beyond it. Alex Comfort in *Sex in Society* suggests the most plausible reason: 'A very important factor in altering the pattern of monogamy and sexual life generally in our society is the change in attitude towards what used to be called "middle age". The years after forty were traditionally viewed by our predecessors as a plateau sloping gradually towards old age, and a time for enjoying what one had, detaching oneself from sexuality and preparing to die content, while deliberately avoiding new experiences in order to facilitate the process. The emotional complications, divorces and love affairs which have always notoriously characterized this age were regarded as evidence of exceptional instability. This stereotype has been fairly thoroughly shattered in our culture, and the years of former incipient stability (or resignation) are now increasingly recognized as a second adolescence leading to a "second chance".'

He goes on to say: 'A culture which prepares itself for a new instalment of life at forty, rather than for the bathchair and the grave, to which on existing vital statistics it is barely half way, needs to make some gesture of recognition towards the change that this implies – we now have two sex-lives, which may be continuous or distinct, and give wider opportunities, both for fulfilment and for

58

making ourselves and others miserable, than the simpler and more compulsive one-shot life-history which used to be the norm. There is thus a strong tendency for married people, even when they have strong ties to their partner, to become involved in sexual exploits outside marriage after it has lasted for some years.'

Lloyd George was an example of a man who needed to have a second strong relationship in his life. He was forty-eight when he met Frances Stevenson, then a twenty-three-year-old teacher, and as mistress and confidential secretary she shared his political life – albeit in the background. She was educated and enlightened, interested in politics and political activities.

While Lloyd George's wife and family remained at either Criccieth in North Wales or his other home at Walton Heath outside London, his secretary was with him helping prepare his speeches, boosting him when he was down, soothing him when he was unwell.

Love meant a great deal to both of them. As she wrote in her diary on 23 April 1917: 'I do not think we have ever loved each other so much. D [Lloyd George] says that ours is a love that comes to very few people and I wonder more and more at the beauty and happiness of it. It is a thing that nothing but death can harm . . .'.

The most common reason why men need to involve themselves in the hugely complicated business of an extra-marital relationship is an unfulfilled need in the marriage.

Elliott Roosevelt, in his book *An Untold Story: The Roosevelts of Hyde Park*, says that his mother, after bearing six children in eleven years, would not have sexual relations with his father: 'Her bland ignorance of how to ward off pregnancy left her no choice except abstinence.'

This disclosure makes more understandable the major revelation in the book: the former President's twenty-two-year relationship with Marguerite (Missy) LeHand, his personal secretary. She died from a stroke in 1944 and F.D.R. died eight months later, but he specified in his will that her medical bills were to be paid by his estate. Elliott wrote: 'I believe he wanted the world to be given some clue to Missy's importance in his life.'

The rest of the family obviously don't share Elliott's views, for in a joint statement F.D.R.'s other four children said they wanted to dissociate themselves from the book. F.D.R. must have had a great need for this second woman in his life since he jeopardized not only his political career but also the happiness of his wife and family.

As in the case of Lloyd George, it was many years before the story of the love was told. It's quite a thought that men who headed powerful nations were in fact challenging the most traditional concepts of their societies – monogamous marriage and the inviolable family unit.

H. G. Wells was married twice, yet in their book *The Time Traveller: The Life of H. G. Wells* Norman and Jeanne MacKenzie suggest that it was just not possible for him to be faithful. His life seemed to hurtle from scandal to scandal, but there must have been a need fulfilled by the infidelities because two of the relationships were long-lasting: with Rebecca West he had a ten-year love affair, and this was followed almost immediately by another ten-year relationship with Odette Keun – she was thirty-six and he was fifty-eight when it started in 1923.

A marriage guidance counsellor we talked to believes that there are large, unfulfilled areas in many marriages. Quite often a husband will find his escape, his withdrawal into a private world, through hobbies – obsessive hobbies which cause him to neglect his wife and family. This is just as much his mistress as a woman would be, but this way his emotions are more secure.

The most common unfulfilled need is sex. But sex is not normally sufficient to sustain a relationship over a long period – the marriage has already shown this. Frequently, in fact, a man is seeking in his extra-marital relationship gratification for a whole series of needs which will vary according to the state of his marriage. If his marriage is shaky, or going through the notorious 'bad spell', then a husband may seek to compensate for the void in his marriage by having an affair.

'For the last seven years I had been getting very restless. We were both increasingly automatic in our responses to each other. We had nothing warm or spontaneous or vital about us. I felt as though she had moved out of a central room in myself and left it empty. My life was sickeningly habitual and routine. I would definitely say if I wasn't actually looking, I was very susceptible to an affair for several years before I actually had one.'

The man in our case history believes he might have been faithful if he'd had children and yet he has a strong need to live life to the full. His affairs keep him young, boost his self-esteem – provide the caviar where others might choose to live on cheese. His marriage suits him, he says it is happy, but to him there is more to life than marriage.

Another lover feels equally strongly:

'If I didn't have affairs I couldn't stay in my marriage. I just can't stay at home. Other women keep my marriage together and they know the score. I don't intend leaving my wife or my children. I never attempt to deceive the women, I tell them straight. If my wife ever found out about me she'd probably have a nervous breakdown. If anybody told her I'd deny it totally – even in a court of law – because she would sit around in a turmoil, utterly

miserable. She's got four children, a beautiful home and she's happy. I'm going to keep her that way.'

This man, immature or not, has a need for sex outside marriage and he's interesting for two reasons: he has no guilt about what he does and sees his relationships as absolutely essential to his and his wife's happiness; and at thirty-two he was the youngest lover we interviewed.

Problems really occur in marriages where the wife has lost her sexual drive, according to the marriage guidance counsellor we spoke to. Quite often when a woman has so much invested in the marriage she will put up with the affairs. The ensuing complication, however, is that once a man realizes the deficiencies he seeks sex outside marriage almost compulsively.

One man we interviewed, who had had his first extra-marital relationship after eleven years of perfunctory to non-existent sex with his wife, had become so addicted to sex after sublimating his sexual potential for so long that he had been involved in a string of affairs ever since. The marriage goes on but he is unable to live a life devoid of sexual satisfaction.

There is obviously a genuine need for some men to have two worlds, one acting as a prop for the other. Quite often, to have the two, the man will need the acquiescence of his wife – and his mistress – if divided loyalties are not to destroy him as a person.

An ingenious way of coming to terms with this came from a dustman in a British town who asked his local council to find him a home big enough for his two families: his wife and their four children, and his mistress and their two children.

He was quoted in the press as saying: 'I am trying to be a good father to all my children. I only earn £25 a week and it's too much of a strain to divide my money and time between two separate households.'

When monogamy remains intact the stunning implication is that it is possible to love two people at the same time, that the loves are complementary and not in conflict with each other. These loves are based on reality, not on fantasy.

6 The Mistress - The Male Fantasy

'My wife and I were always considered a wonderful social match but we just couldn't provide for each other's emotional needs. I decided that because there were children involved the marriage had to continue, but I was determined to find someone else. It sounds calculating and callous but I knew I wanted to find a woman who could give me emotional warmth and not put my marriage in jeopardy.

'I had just about come to the end of the line when I met her. I was quite unable to face up to my home life and she was rather shattered because a relationship she'd had for seven years had just concluded because of the man's infidelity.

'She didn't think much of herself so it's curious that I should have felt attracted to her. I noticed that she was plain and that she looked terribly lost. She wasn't very pleased to learn that I was married but she was prepared to take any kind of second best because of the bad experience she'd had.

'We started to pull each other together almost immediately. My work had got into a terrible state so I used to pay her to come to my office and work three or four nights a week. I could only really work when I knew she would be around. We helped each other – she relieved me from current pressures, and she felt I gave her a great deal of pleasure. I didn't think of the relationship in the long term. I didn't plan ahead because I didn't think that someone as undemanding as she was could keep me involved for very long.

'But I found she fulfilled two roles – she became

sexually important to me and emotionally important. She resembled my grandmother and it was my grandmother who had an enormous influence on my life.

'To be honest I found it glamorous to have a mistress and the fact that I felt it was illegal and wrong added to the excitement. But she was an emotional foil too. She would listen to me all evening. Not like my wife, who was so filled with her own problems that she wouldn't listen to me at all. My mistress was always considerate and put me first.

'I suppose a person with more guts would have left the marriage and moved in with the mistress. But I went on believing in the importance of the marriage and became cowardly about leaving it. All the time, though, it was getting worse and worse. Still I didn't do anything about bringing it to an end. I felt I would have to move in with my mistress and I felt it would be a bad thing for us both for me to go straight from one to the other.

'Sex with my wife had been one of the good things about the marriage. And even though we had other emotional difficulties, the sexual feelings survived. Once I had a mistress I felt even more obliged to put on a better performance – out of guilt. The tiredness made me feel like an old man. I'd have been out with my mistress the whole night and then I'd go and make love to my wife. Then there were the lies I had to tell. Lies about how I'd been too tired to drive home and how I'd spent the night at a friend's. Lying really went against the grain with me and that's really why the truth came out in the end.

'The marriage was finished and it was a relief in a way. But I've had to pay for what's happened.

'My mistress became convinced that I'd been using her because I refused to live with her or marry her after my divorce came through. She had two children by me. She said she didn't expect me to support them but I think for her they were insurance. She thought they would keep me

65

around. Instead I moved into a flat on my own. My wife eventually found out about her and the children but she didn't worry because she'd been having an affair with my best friend for years.

'I see both my former wife and former mistress a lot. They continue to be very demanding. I pay money to both of them for the children so I'm pretty broke most of the time. I had to go to South Africa last year on business and they both turned pretty nasty. They both thought I was going to desert them and that's when I really found out what the cost of being unfaithful is.

'I was wrong to think that a mistress would play just the role I wanted her to play. I never really gave a thought to her needs. My wife was obviously not getting what she wanted from the marriage, or she wouldn't have taken a lover. The marriage itself was wrong and neither her lover nor my mistress caused it to break down.

'I crave for excitement so this makes me basically an unfaithful man. I always feel sure that the grass will be greener somewhere else, with someone else.'

The successful man with a mistress has a great deal of 'unaccountable' time on his hands, endless money (the more the better), a guilt-free conscience, an ability to lie effortlessly and a capacity to live an almost schizophrenic existence. By satisfying two women at the same time, keeping his two worlds apart yet making them both provide what he wants, he is living out a fantasy.

The Alec Guinness film of the '50s, *Captain's Paradise*, which showed him as a sea captain with two wives in different ports, was a comedy of errors because his fantasy worlds were based on the belief that no one changes, that goals and ideals are the same today as they are tomorrow. When the mistress-type wife started to long for domesticity and motherhood, it was a shock to him. When his respectable English mother-type wife expressed a desire for a more flamboyant and less burdened life, the captain's fantasy world evaporated.

The reality is that when the going gets rough, having a mistress is no fantasy at all. In fact most men, if they sat down and thought seriously about it, would probably decide that having a mistress as opposed to having a casual affair just isn't worth the trouble and effort involved.

Two men we interviewed had genuine needs and had two real lives. The other eight – the man in the case history included – were not nearly so positive because their relationships had brought stress and problems that could be solved only by someone suffering. In three cases it was the men themselves, one even going so far as to say that with the wisdom of hindsight he wouldn't, couldn't, go through it all again.

It is obvious that some men enjoy the excitement, the mental dodgings of a double life – to a ludicrous and hilarious extent in one case where the husband had become involved with a new mistress while easing out the old:

'Initially it was a bit awkward. On Christmas Day I had to have three Christmas dinners – one with my family and one with each of my women. None of them realized I'd been anywhere else.'

One quails at the manoeuvrings that must go on in such situations, yet this man thrives. Right from the start of his marriage eight years ago he has sought extra-maritial adventure. He has had two long-term relationships, both with women who worked for him. His wife lives in the country and he has a flat in London where the mistress lives.

'My wife has never found out about my continual affairs. She's never realized that my first mistress lived and worked with me for three years; she doesn't know anything about the present one either. My secret principle is this: I never confess I've been out with a woman. I'll swear I haven't. I'll find excuses if she finds a hair but I've never admitted anything. If you admit it once, it's all over – she'd get suspicious every time I was out. There's not the slightest bit of grey as far as I'm concerned. It's all black and white. Sometimes, I must say, my life becomes terribly complicated, but even when I'm under the most incredible pressure I'll never admit to any of them about other women.'

This man quite enjoys hovering on the edge of a precipice but has no intention whatsoever of jumping over. Others, especially those who are wealthy or who travel a great deal, can escape to a fantasy life.

One mistress involved with a wealthy man describes the relationship as a fairy tale:

'We meet in luxury hotels all over the world. I found the way he lavished money on me embarrassing at first because I wasn't used to it. I am now. We go out to the best and most expensive places, have lavish food, everything. We've only met once in the same country twice. He just rings me and says, "Come to Geneva for the night or New York for a week." It's been fantastic for me. I've got the excitement most people dream of but never have.'

Glamour, exotic places, magnificent splendour – it's all the stuff dreams are made of. It takes flair to make them all come true. And when you're a dedicated fantasist you have to work at it.

'I always keep my relationships very active. We're

always going out, always busy doing something exciting. I never let a relationship get boring, I keep it going the whole time. By putting it on a day-to-day level it gives you something to look forward to tomorrow.'

Money is without doubt the greatest asset for a man wanting to have a fantasy relationship with a mistress. It is costly to raise the pursuit of pleasure above the mundane or ordinary, which is probably why most men would rather dream of having a mistress. She is a perfect dream subject, the ideal companion sexually and emotionally; she's beautiful, titillating, ego-boosting. To have her you must be well-off financially – and as money, and the power it brings, is the other great dream of man, the two are interwoven.

No nine-to-five working man who shares a bank account with his wife is likely to be able to activate a fantasy. Too many times he'll be asked questions, have to account for action he's taken. It is expected that his wife and children will use up most of his free time, and to manage an outside, long-term liaison would require superhuman effort. His ambitions are prescribed, and he's become content with his life simply because to be any different would only confuse and disturb a situation that is satisfying in most ways. While dreams remain fantasies and there is neither an urgent need nor a neurotic impulse to disrupt the pattern, he is happy with his life.

One man told us:

'I couldn't have a mistress. It would be too complicated . . . my old woman takes enough handling as it is. I knew a bloke once who had a mistress for twenty-seven years. He was a very ordinary bloke but because we worked shift patterns, he was able to tell his wife he was working overtime on Saturday afternoon and two nights a week. Then the mistress died and he didn't know what to do

with himself. He couldn't tell his wife the overtime had stopped so he used to come to work and just sit there. He did that for a whole year till he retired. That taught me a lesson about the problems you can get without really trying.'

In living out their fantasies three of the men we interviewed said they made no demands on their mistresses as far as fidelity is concerned. All said that if they discovered their wives were having affairs their reaction would be 'Good for her'.

The others, however, have a double standard – fidelity is not required of them but it is of their mistresses, and of their wives. They regard their mistresses as possessions and their attitudes only underline the inequality of the concept of fidelity. They are seeking, in effect, two simultaneous monogamous relationships. Having abandoned monogamy themselves with no second thoughts or severe doubts, they proceed to judge and demand of their women strict adherence to monogamous values. As one mistress said of her lover:

'He used to say that if Caesar's wife had to be above suspicion, then Caesar's mistress had to be a bloody saint.'

So even a fantasy situation is vulnerable to feelings of insecurity. Presumably this insecurity is intensified by the fact that neither partner in a mistress–lover relationship has got the law on his or her side where demands are concerned, and emotional weapons are needed to secure them to each other.

One mistress made the decision to give up her lover when she learnt of his infidelity.

'I hated sharing him with his wife because I'm not a

*sharing person. But when I became the third one on the
totem pole, I knew it couldn't go on.'*

If the fantasy side brings more pleasure than the
marriage side of a man's life, he may attempt to turn a
dream into a reality by disappearing quietly and abruptly
with his mistress, believing this will free him of all
responsibilities and commitments. The mistress, in effect,
becomes the wife and the wife becomes the outsider – he's
no better off.

Torn between love for his mistress and responsibility to
his family, he can become quite unable to make a decision
either way. The man in our case history, for example, had
this problem. He was being stretched on a rack and his
response was to flee to South Africa. But the problems
were still there when he returned. He couldn't dream
them away.

Another lover, having insisted to his mistress that his
marriage was in ruins (and it was), said that he couldn't
live without her. For the next eighteen years he oscillated
helplessly from ultimatum to ultimatum and crisis to crisis
with his mistress and his wife. When the two women got
together after all the promises and postponements they
discovered he had been adamantly insisting to his wife
that he wasn't going to leave home (and was going to end
the affair), while to his mistress he insisted he was going to
leave home (and his wife). Had his mistress not finally
given up in despair – her trust and faith in him eroded by
prevarication and dissembling – he would probably have
continued in this state of indecision indefinitely.

A fantasy cannot last. By its very nature it is short-lived
and, as it did for the captain in paradise, reality bursts the
dream bubble. The implications of a fantasy can be only
expectations as insubstantial as gossamer – and as one
mistress said, 'Life's just not like that.'

7 The Mistress - the Power Behind the Scenes

'I can honestly say I have never regretted not being married. I think I have reaped far more rewards being a mistress than I would ever have had as a wife. In a material sense I am very well off, I can go where I want when I want and there is no one preventing me being myself.

'When you've been involved in a relationship as long as I have, looking back to how it started is like asking an old married woman to remember her courting days. I know that I wasn't like the girls I went to school with. They wanted only to be married and to have children. I was never interested in either of these, but I think I assumed I would get married one day.

'I came from a very small Welsh village and I wanted more than anything to get away from it. I taught myself shorthand and typing and moved to Cardiff where I got a job in a factory. I was nineteen and I stayed there for two years. A big London firm took over the business and when one of the bosses asked if I'd like to join the staff there I jumped at the chance.

'I'd only been working there about six months when I was transferred to the director's suite – and that's where I've been ever since. No, *I'm* not a director, but in decision-making terms I have the same power.

'The director I went to work for was ten years older than me and I became used to being more than just a secretary. I used to arrange his cocktail parties, act as hostess when necessary, go with him to other cities on business trips. Right from the start I'd realized that I was attracted to his way of life, and I was attracted to him.

'We started going out to dinner when we'd worked late and then when we went to Birmingham for a conference, we began sleeping together. His wife had been away for several weeks at their cottage in France but I don't think that was the reason we slept together. We were a good working team and we both felt quite natural spending out-of-work hours together.

'Gradually I started taking decisions for him when he was away from the office. I not only composed his letters, I started signing them as well – I knew instinctively he would agree with whatever decision I'd made. They weren't earth-shattering decisions but quite important for the firm.

'I'd been living in a small flat and my boss insisted that I get a larger one and the firm would take care of the rent. This worked out well for it was not only used for small business dinners but it also gave my lover and me a meeting place. I liked playing hostess at those dinners. It meant no work for me because a caterer did it all. As the dinners were usually for visiting businessmen, I was the only woman there and I enjoyed it.

'I was continually getting rises in pay so I could afford to buy really good clothes and each year I started taking two weeks' holiday in first-class hotels. France was the place I liked best because there was usually at least two unattached men who would be able to take me to dinner, sailing or sightseeing.

'The love affair with my boss continued to develop. He was very attached to me emotionally but he also needed me as part of his job. I met his wife quite frequently and we got on well. She only came up to London to shop or meet friends. She had her own life but she got what she wanted out of the marriage. Her sons were all at boarding school so she had a lot of freedom.

C*

'At one time my lover became very guilty about the affair. He felt he wasn't doing right either by his wife or by me and he wanted to get a divorce and marry me. I felt that would be very silly because I was already seeing more of him than she was and I certainly had all the influence over him I wanted. It took him a while to understand that as I considered myself his wife there was no need to have a legal tie. We both knew that if I became his wife I wouldn't be able to go on working for him and that I would be relegated to the house in the country. It certainly wouldn't suit me, and I convinced him that it wouldn't suit him either. He genuinely did do a lot of travelling around and I just couldn't be a wife who sat and waited.

'We are always circumspect at the hotels wherever we go. We both have double rooms but usually adjoining or nearby. I like being with him, it makes me feel important. We never get bored in each other's company because we have so much in common. We share much more than we ever would in a marriage.

'On several occasions I've met other businessmen who travel with their personal assistants. They seem so much younger than I am and I get the feeling that these women would all like to be the wife. I'd like to take them aside and tell them to hold on tight to what they have because being a wife will only mean loneliness. Perhaps I might have wished to marry if I'd wanted children. But I am too married to my job and my boss to want children. They would only have upset a perfect situation.'

The only thing that can't be disproved about the mistress historically is the power she wielded. Emma Hamilton came close to changing the course of history – she almost held Nelson back from Trafalgar.

And Madame Pompadour, mistress of Louis XV,

certainly had power and influence for twenty years as 'the uncrowned Queen of France'. A brilliant woman, interested in both the arts and politics, at one time she ran most of the internal business of France from her royal apartments.

From bourgeois French origins she had been educated to her role by a clever and determined mother. Physically she had all the ingredients for success: she was attractive to look at, slim and elegant, charming and vivacious. After making a fortunate 'social' marriage, her strategy led her to be installed as the royal mistress in 1745. She stayed in the King's favour until she died.

She is most probably the archetypal example of a mistress who wielded power behind the scenes. She stayed in power through her cleverness, knowing best how to keep the King amused and when she shouldn't over-step her position. It has been said that she herself was frigid, but this didn't affect her power. *She* chose the women for the King's bed and, in pleasing the sexually robust Louis this way, she retained her influence.

Intelligent and talented Pompadour would undoubtedly have been a success if she had lived at any stage in history.

The woman in our case history, like Pompadour, turned the situation to her own advantage, enjoyed the role she found for herself and worked only towards making herself indispensable, certainly irreplaceable as far as her lover was concerned. Having come to rely on his mistress and not being put in any position where he would feel guilty, a man would be reluctant to alter the situation.

One can only speculate about how much power Marguerite (Missy) LeHand had where Franklin D. Roosevelt was concerned. She was his mistress (according to his son Elliott Roosevelt's book *An Untold Story: The Roosevelts of Hyde Park*) when he was governor of New

York and when he was President of the United States – covering a period of about twenty-two years.

In the son's words, Missy became F.D.R.'s 'shield, nurse and outspoken friend' and soon 'shared a completely familial existence with Father.' At the Governor's mansion, the son wrote, 'Father had the . . . bedroom next to Missy's. These two rooms were joined by a little door with clear glass panels curtained on her side . . . Mother thought that this was a perfectly suitable arrangement.'

Elliott Roosevelt related how it was 'not unusual to enter Father's sunny corner room and find Missy there in her nightgown. There was no attempt to conceal their relationship . . . "Missy is my conscience", Father used to say with no sense of irony.'

The arrangement continued in the White House where Missy had her own apartment 'assigned to her by Mother'.

One cannot imagine that affairs of State were never discussed because Roosevelt was a political being and someone as close as Missy must have been involved in preliminary thought before decisions were taken.

In Britain, Lloyd George's relationship with his private secretary Frances Stevenson was respected even by his 'bitterest opponents', according to A. J. P. Taylor in *Lloyd George: A Diary By Frances Stevenson*. Frances Stevenson took a degree in classics at London University and then taught in a girls' boarding school. She was employed to teach Lloyd George's daughter Megan in the summer holidays. That was in 1911. In 1912 Lloyd George invited her to become a secretary at the treasury 'on his own terms which were in direct conflict with my essentially Victorian upbringing', as she wrote in *The Years That Are Past*.

At Christmas 1912 she accepted these terms, and so began a relationship that ended only with Lloyd George's death.

76

He was Chancellor of the Exchequer when she became his secretary. He took over the Ministry of Munitions from 1915 to July 1916 and was appointed Secretary of War from July to December 1916. On 7 December 1916 he headed the Coalition Government and remained in power as Prime Minister until 1922.

Frances Stevenson not only loved Lloyd George, she also shared his political interests and was, according to A. J. P. Taylor, soon at home in the great world of public affairs. She was an efficient secretary and also helped Lloyd George compose his speeches. She went with him on important foreign missions and met all the important statesmen of the day. On Lloyd George's behalf she negotiated with the press lords, Northcliffe and Beaverbrook – and she wrote down everything she heard. Because of this she is of great value to the political historian.

Lloyd George and Frances Stevenson did not marry until 1943 – two years before he was created Earl. He died just two months later. For all the important years of his life Frances Stevenson had played a powerful role, a role that even a wife could not play. She was always on hand to listen, to praise, even to give advice when asked.

In her diary dated 20 November 1914, she wrote: 'C [her reference to Lloyd George as Chancellor] again referred to the love letters he sent me two years ago, when he was wooing me ... they were indeed very beautiful but the things he says to me now are more beautiful still. Sometimes I am so happy that I tremble for fear it will not last. Our love will always last, but there is the dread that he might be taken from me. He is never tired of talking of that summer when he asked to come to Allenswood, and we both felt there was something between us, though it was not yet expressed; and of the following autumn when we used to meet once a week, and I hovered between doubt and longing dread and desire; and of the time in the

House of Commons when I left him because I would not agree to his proposals, but returned soon after to say that I could not face life without him . . . I have never regretted the decision. It has brought me two years of happiness and if fate wills will bring me many more.'

Lloyd George was twenty-five years older than Frances Stevenson – he married his first wife, Margaret Owen, in the year Frances was born, 1885. He had two sons and three daughters. The passage of his love for Frances did not run smoothly. Frances expressed a little of the trouble in her diary dated 11 March 1915: 'My people have been trying to separate us – trying to make me pronounce that I will give up his love, the most precious thing of my life. They do not understand – they will never understand – they do not see our love is pure and lasting – they think I am his plaything and that he will fling me aside when he has finished with me – or else they think that there will be a scandal and that we shall all be disgraced.'

It was never to happen. The relationship flourished and she remained by his side in a position of trust and understanding. She knew as well as anybody of the power politics that were being played, yet rarely was she seen in public with Lloyd George. She was able to remain in the background – because of the discretion of her lover's friends.

Lady Jennie Churchill was not so fortunate. She has established a place in history for her pursuit of power – for her husband and her son – through her lovers. As the beautiful American wife of Lord Randolph Churchill, society was opened to her and she took advantage of the situation where she could.

As another famous woman of the times, Lily Langtry, was influential in entertainment, Jennie Churchill was influential in politics – not in the way that perhaps Barbara Castle is in the Labour Party today, but as somebody who knew the right people and whose views were respected. Her marriage became one of social convenience simply because of Sir Randolph's syphilitic condition. As Ralph G. Martin, Lady Jennie's biographer, says: there was an unspoken arrangement; Jennie could have her suitors, Randolph his friends.

She played a valuable role in her husband's political life, helping to write his speeches, campaigning round the country for him. She was the unrecognized fifth member of the political group called the Fourth Party, which consisted of Lord Randolph, Arthur Balfour, Sir Henry Wolff and John Gorst. Not only was she favoured by a future prime minister, she was also entertained by a future king. Prince Edward gave her expensive jewellery and invited her to be a frequent guest at Sandringham – and Randolph did not always accompany her.

While George Nathaniel Curzon (he became viceroy of India) allegedly fell in love with her, and Sir Charles Dilke was said to have gone down on his knees and begged her to be his mistress, Jennie's major interest in love was the Austrian count Charles Rudolf Ferdinand Kinsky, a man four years younger than she. He had a reputation for woman-chasing, as did another of her long-term friends Herbert von Bismarck, son of the German chancellor.

When Lord Randolph finally succumbed to the debilitating disease, Lady Jennie concentrated on helping her son Winston, and on one occasion she invited to lunch Rosebery, Balfour and Asquith, all of whom helped to shape Winston's future. As Ralph G. Martin wrote in the second volume of the biography, she would 'tap the men and open the doors to prepare the complicated pattern of stepping stones to his future.'

From our interviews it would seem that some modern mistresses want to find involvement with whatever business their lovers are in. Three of the mistresses inter-

viewed experienced power in this way – and learnt from
it.

*'I came to know everything there is to know about
publishing. For ten years he used to discuss his problems
with me and I often helped him make up his mind about a
book he wasn't sure about. He was very successful as a
publisher and I know that he never discussed his work
with his wife. Just with me.'*

Only when this relationship ended did this mistress
turn the knowledge she gained to her own advantage.
With his help she established a firm with interests allied
to publishing.

Another mistress who had lived with a writer for
several years started helping him with his work because
she was interested in it. His was a specialist field and she
discovered she was better than he at expressing his
thoughts.

*'We established a routine: I wrote two books for him,
did all his typing, wrote his lectures. In fact I earned
quite a lot of our money. I even helped to support his
wife. I don't think at the beginning he meant to use me
but we became such a good partnership that he wanted it
to go on.'*

When her lover's infidelity brought the liaison to an
end, the mistress kept up her professional attachment to
her former lover; they have now established a business
and, although as a ghost writer she doesn't receive any
more recognition than in the past, she certainly benefits
financially.

Airlines is the name of the game for a twenty-six-year-
old P.R.O. and her lover. This mutual interest gave them
a base for the advancement of their affair which had

started out as 'a little fling'. They found themselves at the same international centres and gradually they became more involved with each other.

'He's very wealthy, very powerful and highly respected. I was extremely flattered by his attention. He told me he could offer me job security, love, money – everything except marriage. And this would continue whether or not I got married.'

For this mistress the future holds a business partnership with her lover. And she accepts the limitations of the relationship.

'He won't let our feelings for each other get in the way of work. He will never rearrange a meeting to see me. Sometimes I don't see him till the early hours of the morning because to him business comes first.'

However, there are advantages. Because they have the same work interest they can spend work hours together and her position is recognized.

'We go out openly with his friends and business associates because it's accepted in these circles. When we go out with clients they're mostly with their own mistresses anyway. I'm more surprised in this business to find someone who's not involved than to meet someone with another woman.'

She has been quick to realize that a liaison with such a powerful man can be only for her good. Knowing him has increased not only her self-esteem but also her esteem in the eyes of her employers.

'They all know about me and I see them looking at me and thinking, "If she can get this man she must have something."'

Wherever women can reap rewards in the power game, the mistress must be temperamentally complementary to her lover. Her understanding of his business world, her recognition of his role and her devotion to his progress enable her to establish a beneficial partnership that is often more valuable than a marriage would be.

By accepting this path, however, she must expect a certain amount of loneliness. She has little time in which to have a life of her own – everything she does is directed towards her lover. She must subordinate her own needs to his; his goals must also be hers.

'Being a mistress to a businessman is a funny, parasitic state. Because you're emotionally and physically interested in this one man, you change your life-pattern to his.'

But the man goes to his own life, to his wife and family, and it's then that the mistress is left to her own resources and is exposed to her own unfulfilled needs.

'Loneliness gets to bug you. You sit in on a Saturday night cooling your heels watching yet another TV movie. I was emotionally dependent on my lover and because we were so close I wasn't getting to meet other people at all. I felt I was vegetating, becoming an old woman at twenty-eight.'

This mistress had reached a powerful position in a New York firm, yet an urge to test her own potential led her to break with her lover, leave America and come to London. The knowledge she gained through her relationship with her lover has enabled her to be a success in a job here. Now she wields power in her own right.

Some mistresses are content to stay behind the scenes, as the mistress in our case history is. All her needs are met in her relationship with her employer-lover. Only when she feels restrained or restricted by her role will she seek power elsewhere. Like Pompadour, she turns her learning to her advantage, but unlike Pompadour she will never have the same power. That type of mistressing has gone for ever.

8 The Mistress - The Predator

'I have a very basic attitude – I've been used so often by men that it's my turn to use them. I will only go out with a man who can be of use to me, who can assist me with my career. I'm a late-starting journalist so I only go for men who are right at the top. At my age starting on a lower rung would be a waste of time. As every editor I've ever met is married, I have to become a mistress to them. The one-night stand has no value, as I'm not doing this for sex.

'My strategy at the beginning was quite simple. When I moved from California to New York I had press accreditation from quite an influential paper for whom I had been doing freelance work. In New York I just went through the telephone book ringing the editors of all the newspapers listed. I told them I wanted to interview them. I've found that everyone – successful men especially – like to be interviewed. They feel flattered. If they sounded at all hesitant I would say, "I think you should meet me. I'm quite attractive." It never failed. They expected a femme fatale and they got one. I swept into the interviews and set about impressing them. In the course of the interview I would mention that I was looking for a job and they almost always responded. I was given special treatment.

'I decided I would try and seduce the most handsome and influential of the men I interviewed – and the most responsive one, of course. I singled out just one. We had only two meals together before I became his mistress.

'I'd worked out how to play the game. I knew how to subtly imply there were other lovers (and there were) to make him jealous and competitive – I have a sneaking suspicion that this is the only hunting spirit left in men like this. I knew how to imply I was more successful than I was. I name-dropped furiously and in the beginning manoeuvred every situation. It worked. Within five months of arriving in New York I was living in a magnificent flat and I had two men helping me. The flat is paid for by my married lover of four years standing from California, but I'm being kept by my other lover. He knows that someone else exists in my life but not that he's paying for my flat. My flat is really luxurious and it gives me importance and adds mystery as far as my new lover is concerned.

'I intend keeping the relationship going until I am well established. At the moment my lover makes sure I get all my articles published. I'll gradually meet other men, find other outlets, but in the meantime I'm sitting pretty.

'I'm carefully collecting contacts. I'm not promiscuous – that way men use you. No, my style is to flirt madly with influential men and tantalize them as much as I can. Only long-standing relationships will help me benefit careerwise.

'Why did I start out doing this? Because I've been married twice and both times I have been badly hurt. One of them left me for another woman, and both left me without any money. The second marriage was a pure mistake – he gave me nothing, physically, emotionally or financially. I was pretty miserable for a while and then I got mad. I took a long hard look at myself.

'The only assets I had, I realized, was myself. I had intelligence and good looks on my side. I certainly didn't look thirty-eight. I completely discounted any idea of taking a minor secretarial job or even trying to join a local paper. I was determined that I was going to get the best job and, like an ad-man, I set out to sell myself. I guess I really regarded myself as a product and I was a first-class saleswoman because I had everything to gain.

'I know that if I hadn't gone about it the way I did, I wouldn't be where I am now. I don't feel at all guilty about it because long ago I realized that it was only because I was a woman that I had to go about establishing a career this way. I have nothing of my own so I must get what I want from men.

'If I had been a man I would have had a good education and I wouldn't have spent eleven years as a housewife, wasting all my talents. I consider I am getting my just deserts. I am a women's liberation supporter though I don't actively participate in the movement. I think we women have got to use every available weapon if we're going to get out of our subordinated condition. I've done it all on my own – by using the only resource I have – and presumably I've given my lovers something as well or they wouldn't have hung around for so long and wouldn't have given me so much in return. I enjoy this new attitude. It means I'm always winning, instead of losing as I did for all the years I was married.'

The cold, hard, calculating mistress does exist. She's alive and prospering, using men as vehicles to give her all she wants. She's not a run-of-the-mill mistress in any sense. She's made a conscious decision about her role and she's willing to commit herself fully to it for the rewards alone.

She is the most exotic of the mistresses and she uses her wiles and her body to insinuate her way into the lives of wealthy men, men with power, men who can raise her status. She plans her romances with as much attention to detail as a general contemplating the capture of an enemy.

As a mistress she draws up her own code of ethics. Her

greatest quality is her sense of self-discipline, her concentration on her own self-advancement. She works hard at making the most of her looks, at being charming and graceful. She is always impeccably dressed and has developed her talents in the male-praised social arts of hostessing and listening.

Unlike the more usual mistress she doesn't allow herself to fall in love – she'd never be so susceptible. Her emotions are involved only to the extent that she knows how best to use them for effect.

Her tactics are well thought out, for she's playing for big stakes. She aims at perfecting herself according to her own high standards, for the more perfect she is the more chance there will be of a bigger return.

She is a predator in the sense that she cannot exist alone, only in conjunction with a goal to be achieved. Everything, every action in her life, is directed to that purpose. With her eye firmly fixed on tomorrow she taps her conquests for gifts that appreciate in value – jewellery, shares, real estate and houses. These considerable material rewards of the predator are often the result of guilt, a compensation for the lovers' feelings of using the mistresses to their own ends.

Marion Davies was set up by brilliant American Randolph Hearst in the palatial San Simeon residence, showered with gifts for the twenty-five years of the relationship. The silent-screen star might have suffered from not having her situation legalized in marriage, but, as many people at the time were swift to point out, she certainly got a lot out of the years. Coming as she did from a fairly humble background, Marion the chorus girl was lifted out of her modest existence and placed in a fantasy world. She did have talent, and Hearst brought out of her talents she didn't know existed where business was concerned, but she would probably have remained in the chorus line-up if she hadn't been so determined to better herself. Her affair with one of America's most influential and wealthy men was the opportunity of a lifetime.

The most common characteristic of the more famous – or infamous – mistresses of history is the way they have maintained power over their lovers long after the sexual side had waned. Having built up their lovers' reliance on them, they planned to hold on for all their worth.

Pompadour was certainly never completely in control of Louis XV, but she knew how to pamper him, to be the object on which he could be extravagant. Luckily for France her persistence and attitudes of self-advancement left a priceless legacy of works of art – she was responsible for helping to establish the porcelain factories at Sèvres which rivalled the already famous Dresden.

Britain too had strong women with self-interest. Lady Conyngham, mistress to George IV, was thought by early nineteenth-century contemporaries to have no brains. Perhaps they were hidden by her shrewdness. Through her kingly liaison her husband was promoted to high office, and they lived completely at the King's expense. It was said that she spent half the time during the King's last and fatal illness praying for his recovery and the other half packing up the furniture to take with her when her days at Windsor would be over. She saw this as the rewards of her devotion.

Using relationships to get into circles where a good marriage is likely is not an uncommon occurrence. Nancy Parsons was a woman who moved from one rich protector to another – British Prime Minister Lord Grafton and the Duke of Dorset – until she acquired a lordly husband. Her charm and intelligence attracted many more admirers, but she had her official standing and she kept it.

The Spider Lady, Lola Montez, most probably tops the list in shock-value terms. England, France, Germany,

America, Australia – everywhere she went she left behind stories of men spellbound by her, seemingly against their will.

This voluptuous dancer was ruthless in her pursuit of fame and fortune. She wasn't, as she said, Spanish, but the daughter of a poor English soldier. She had but one aim and that was to catch a prince. And she did – Ludwig I of Bavaria. She gained so much political power (and, more important, instituted reforms in a very backward country) that her lover, under pressure from his court, was forced to banish her.

Undeterred she set off through the goldfields of California and Australia, dancing her erotic dance in which small rubber spiders fell from her very sparse clothing. When, two husbands later, she returned to Europe, the deposed Ludwig made an honest woman of her for the third time. But she didn't stay with him long and went back to America where she died of syphilis.

These women had no other choice than to be mistresses. Finding the right lover and protector was their main chance – men ruled everything, decided everything, and only by using them could women reach the top. Their good looks and personalities were their fortunes, their passports to a comfortable life.

Today women can achieve so much in their own right, but more often than not they can be helped by the right liaisons.

'I knew that through him I could find a whole new way of life that I would find difficult getting involved in. He introduced me to an enormous number of interesting, useful people who helped me when I left university. I had no wish to break up his marriage, just to get launched in my new career.'

Another mistress we interviewed confessed to blatantly

using her lovers for her own self-advancement. She goes out exclusively with the wealthiest men in London, all of whom so far have been married. She believes that only they can help her find *la dolce vita*. Holidays in the south of France, the Bahamas and Miami – her year's activities sound like a travel-brochure. She has had four affairs, three of them lasting more than two years, and they ended only because the patronage began to be less than forthcoming. She admitted to choosing her partners in terms of their ability to support her high standard of living.

In this attitude she resembles the Victorian kept woman who believed in being a financial parasite – with just one difference. The Victorian woman usually had no other means of support. This mistress simply does not choose to try.

Money played a part in the life of one of the mistresses we interviewed to such an extent that it gave her a new philosophy. Now in her middle twenties, she's on her second long-term affair but she has bitter memories of the lengths one man went to in her life.

'*At eighteen I was very naïve. I was working in my first job as a secretary when my boss told me that if I slept with him I could get a promotion. He said if I didn't he'd sack me and tell the agency that I'd stolen money. I was so scared of him that I agreed. He was just using me. I eventually wrote a letter to the managing director – anonymously of course – and the bastard got the sack. He was always threatening me and I turned the tables on him. He taught me one thing – no man will ever use me again.*'

Whether out of revenge or cunning, the predator-type mistress acts on her own behalf and gives new insight into the casting-couch legend. It has been assumed that men originated this for their own ends, but the predator knows how to exploit it. The communications field – acting, journalism, television and broadcasting – seem the most vulnerable to this practice (as the woman in our case history bears out). We spoke to a self-confessed mistress in each group, but not one was willing to answer our questionnaire. An unusually reticent actress told us coolly, 'I have nothing to gain from talking to you.'

The BBC is always accused of being a hotbed of something or other, and while rumours abound and stories were told to us, we could not get one mistress to talk to us. One secretary told us that she'd got a job there because she'd been told that's where you get the best sexual experience. She was enjoying herself but she hardly fitted what we were looking for!

There is no doubt that as women increasingly come to consider their careers and self-interest first, they will increasingly assess relationships in terms of how they will benefit them. But it would be misleading to categorize all women who have such feelings as predators, for, after all, they are only doing what men have been expected to do all along.

It is only the cynical, embittered women who repress their emotions in the name of advancement, or who choose a man simply for his parasite potential, who can properly be called predators.

9 The Mistress - The Scarlet Woman

'My heart really went out to Lord Lambton when he was found out. You can go on for ages doing things that are frowned upon, but it's only when you are caught out that the trouble really starts. I must have been very naïve, I think. I'd had two affairs with married men, and they had started and finished without anyone being in any way aware that anything was amiss. Order was not disturbed, as they say.

'With my third affair it was different. I fell in love and he loved me in return. The problem was that he was a major public figure and I was a threat to his future importance. We had six very glorious months before the rumours about us started. We'd been seen somewhere together and "a very good friend" had rung up his wife to tell her.

'I knew all along it was a mistake to go out openly. I had accepted at the beginning that the relationship had to be clandestine, but my lover couldn't bear to have his life prescribed. He said his marriage was finished anyway and that he and his wife were only together because of the children, and because as a prospective MP, people preferred you to be married. As far as the voters were concerned, it didn't matter if the marriage were rotten.

'His wife took the news very badly. She may not have been getting on well with her husband, but she had a position to keep up and she had been offended that he didn't feel the same way.

'The next few months were a nightmare. She started spreading rumours about me – she knew who I was but we'd never met. As fast as my friends would deny that I had illegitimate children, that I had been married before, that I was a known prostitute, a new rumour would have started. There was no way of countering them all apart from taking an ad. in the local paper and that would have meant playing her game.

'I started to feel very self-conscious, paranoiac, about this woman rumour had created. Perhaps I really was a terrible person. I felt guilty that I was in love and I was uncertain about what I should do. The decision was made for me by the people I worked for. I was asked to find another job. Just like that, with no reason given. I found out later that it had been my lover's agent who had arranged the sacking. He felt I was a threat to the party, that the seat would change hands at the election if the relationship continued.

'My lover was furious when he heard. He felt he should be judged by his political effectiveness, not as a lover or husband. He tried very hard to persuade the agent otherwise but it was no use. My lover dug in his heels and insisted that we start going out much more together. From now on he wouldn't hide at all. It shattered me. I tried very hard for his sake but I was always aware of people looking at me, the whispers, the pointed fingers.

'I started getting phone calls – people accusing me of being all sorts of things. Mostly the accusers were women, and they didn't sound young. Once, when I was walking along the street, a woman who worked in the party office came up to me and started shouting abuse. She must have felt very strongly or she wouldn't have chosen such a public place. Normally she was a mild-mannered woman but to me she was a shrew. I ran away from her, in tears.

'That was it, I decided. I couldn't go on with this. I couldn't hope to continue a relationship with such violent opposition from all sides. My lover tried to stop me but I had had a year of unhappiness and that was no way to sustain a relationship. We'd begun to bicker over small things and this was just our way of showing the strain we felt. I had to get away so I got a job in a town about fifty miles away.

'I had six weeks' break before my lover started visiting me. We were still in his constituency and should have known that his presence in the town would not go unnoticed. The phone calls began again so I had the phone taken out. Then came the letters – all signed, so no one was worried about keeping their identities secret. That they would run the risk of being sued for slander (and I had grounds, for the letters were filled with terrible, derogatory statements – all untrue) convinced me that I was fighting a force beyond me.

'I moved right away. I'm still in love with my lover and we have met twice in the last year. He's been shaken by it too and we're better off not seeing each other until we can decide what he wants to do. He believes he should divorce but he's very attached to his children and doesn't want to lose them. His wife has told him that she won't let him see them again if he pursues the idea of divorce.

'What makes me feel so cross is that I am unable to help him. I should be by his side, supporting him. But I haven't the courage. I have been branded by society for falling in love and I can't face up to the continual accusations. With any luck his career won't suffer and perhaps if he gets through the next election, he'll be confident enough to go ahead with divorce. I suppose then it will all come out again about us but by that time my wounds might have healed and I'll be strong enough to cope.'

We've all heard references to the mistress as a scarlet woman, a temptress, a sorceress, a seducer of innocent victims, a cold, calculating bitch who lures responsible men from the family hearth and breaks up marriages with irresponsible abandon.

All these clichés have an unconcealed double standard. They assume there is no code of ethics to judge a mistress by, and quite another for the married man. The mistress is judged, and judged harshly, while the married man is forgiven his waywardness on the grounds that he was led astray.

The mistress is the one, like Eve, who leads the man, Adam, to sin. As the Bible insists: it is just and right that she should be considered guilty for leading innocent Adam to sin.

The very word 'mistress' reeks of a double standard. Only an adulterous woman is thus labelled to describe her crime. The adulterous male has no label. He is simply described as a mistress's lover. Her crime, the word implies, is always greater.

What emerges very blatantly from a study of the mistress today is the one-sidedness of our notion of fidelity and the inequality of the Christian concept of adultery. Man the adulterer is spared social disapproval, the ignominy of labels, the burden of guilt. These are reserved (unless a man is an eminent public figure) for the female adulterer who becomes the scapegoat for social outrage and abuse. She is the one who can never escape the social responsibility for the crime (adultery) that she and her lover commit jointly in their illicit relationship.

The origins of such hypocrisy are deeply buried in history, particularly Christian history. It is because of our contact with Christian teaching in our formative years that it is not surprising that these hypocritical attitudes should be accepted so unquestioningly – by women as much as men.

Beginning with the assumptions of Adam's innocence and Eve's guilt, Christianity has consistently emphasized woman's unworthiness and fickleness, man's superiority and moral probity. Particularly from the time of Gregory IV, when celibacy was imposed, the Church proclaimed that women are dangerous and sorcerous. Their seductive guile, it was feared, would distract men from their lofty missions; therefore they were to be avoided. Celibacy became the heroic condition.

In Revelations St John, referring it is thought to Rome at that time, said he saw a vision of a woman 'arrayed in purple and scarlet colour' sitting upon a scarlet-coloured beast. Upon her head were written the words 'Babylon the Great, the mother of Harlots and abominations of the Earth'. Hence the origins of the term 'scarlet woman'.

St John, in his disgust for her, effectively added to the structure of sexual inequality and hypocrisy that we are still encumbered by today. The double standard has been reinforced through the ages – particularly in the Puritan period when men, in whose hands and minds morality was entrusted, were obsessed with woman's supposed powers of seduction and witchery. The retribution on the woman who, in terms of the time, 'sinned' was so horrific that it must have made all women wonder if they were not cursed creatures.

A modern mistress may not be burned at the stake or physically tortured, but she does suffer from the social pressures, particularly if her affair becomes public knowledge. Few women readily accept the description of themselves as mistresses, because it seems to make explicit the fact that they are doing something wrong.

Even fewer women accept the position of a mistress easily, without guilt and self-blame. For the tragedy of most mistresses is that they judge themselves as harshly as they expect society to judge them. At best they uneasily rationalize what they are doing.

'I do feel terrible guilt about it, but, as with religion, you push the guilt to the back of your mind. You close your mind to it because you know you're getting what you need at the time.'

Right from the beginning of a relationship most mistresses accept that they cannot declare their feelings in public. They feel it would somehow be regarded as shameful, and would cause them to be social outcasts. Most still accept that they have to be hidden away, and meetings with their lovers must be clandestine. They meet only when their lovers arrange it, at a meeting place invariably well away from anyone who could recognize them.

'You become furtive and paranoiac about meeting. My heart used to beat awfully fast when I was going to see him; then I realized it was fear that we might be seen, that someone would tell his wife he was having an affair. I knew too that my friends would be scornful of me for having anything to do with a married man.'

Because of the nagging feeling that she is committing a crime by loving the wrong man, she tends to accept public disapproval as the price she must pay for what she's doing. She has no public means to fight back anyway, so she endures contempt, ostracism, hostility and anger silently and bravely, believing these to be her 'just deserts'.

We are well conditioned to the idea of monogamy and the assumption of sexual inequality on which it is based, so few will openly rebel and fight the hostility and disapproval they feel all around them. Christine Keeler and Mandy Rice-Davis (who were admittedly involved in one of the more outlandish scandals of our time) learnt to their cost what happens when you try to explain or justify your actions. Lady Emma Hamilton has paid the price too, in historical terms. Her biographers are generally agreed that she was a bright, obviously attractive and intelligent woman, yet she will be remembered more for the Terence Rattigan film version of her romance in

Bequest to a Nation, where she was portrayed as a drunken, loud-mouthed bitch. Probably most people would rather think of her like that, rather than as a heroic woman standing up against society for the man she loved.

The mistress is a woman without apologists or supporters. In public terms she is *persona non grata—an* isolated woman living on the fringes of society, neither recognized by nor integrated in it.

'Society knows we exist. They know we're here but people don't like to admit it. Obviously the very fact that we exist in such large numbers means we're fulfilling, like the prostitute, a tremendous need. That in itself justifies our existence.'

Whether they resent it or not, the majority of mistresses have to pretend they don't exist. They have to accept that their lovers deny their existence – at least to wives and colleagues, though not perhaps to close male friends.

A mistress has to accept that she is the one who is shunned and hidden away while her lover enjoys the privileges of normal social intercourse of which she is deprived. Society might choose, retrospectively, to mythicize her and make films about her, but while she is alive and well and threatening, she simply does not exist. Because she doesn't exist you can't expect society to collect any statistics about her.

Women are often the severest critics of the mistress – understandably, for she represents a very real threat, particularly to wives who are uncertain about the strength of their own marriages. A mistress who is found out often becomes, as a consequence, a scapegoat for almost every wife's fears and anxieties, and she will probably find herself subjected to astonishingly vindictive hostility. She may find herself, as did the woman in the case history, transformed in the public mind into a treacherous, unscrupulous, ruthless, stereotype scarlet woman, while in reality she is vulnerable, confused and horrified.

This exaggerated condemnation reflects the Freemasonry of married people and their hypocritical attitude: it doesn't matter how much the single girl is hurt, just as long as nothing is allowed to endanger the married state. The feelings of most mistresses are consequently almost never considered by the married couples, and particularly by the sorority of wives. They often consider she deserves no sympathy or understanding at all simply because of her non-married status.

Ordinary wifely fears and anxieties over whether husbands are liable to have mistresses are compounded by feelings of envy and jealousy. The mistress is seen to represent everything many wives obviously lack – glamour, freedom, irresponsibility. Standing over her sink in the morning, many a wife must secretly fantasize a glamorous relationship, such as she imagines every mistress must have.

They will dream about a time when they are free from all the responsibilities of child-rearing, when they are loved and desired as real sex objects instead of being taken for granted as domestic drudges.

If a wife, dreaming such fantasies, feels herself rather to be chained to the sink and distinctly unglamorous, then she will probably feel resentful and inadequate. A 'discovered' mistress, for this woman, will easily become a convenient victim on which she can vent feelings of rage and anger at the injustice of the whole social situation.

None is so vengeful as the 'wronged wife'. Wives, supported by the sorority, seem to feel that any action, any slander or vilification of the mistress is entirely justifiable. Some would indulge in the most unloving, nasty

99

behaviour and justify it all in the name of 'love' for the husband.

We found a newspaper story which showed to what lengths a wife will go. In Vienna a woman found pictures of another woman in her husband's wallet. Recognizing the nude girl as her supposed best friend, she had each of the photographs blown up to poster size and pasted them up around the city with captions like 'Behold the adulteress' and 'Lock up your man when you see this woman'. She ended up in court on a charge of displaying obscene photographs and was given a token five days' imprisonment. When she came out of prison she was reconciled with her husband.

'Hell hath no fury like a woman scorned' is a platitude which retains contemporary significance. Apart from the wife in the case study who publicly slandered the mistress, six mistresses commented on the revengeful treatment they received from their lovers' wives. One said:

'The wife thought I was a temptress, a sorcerer, and nothing would convince her that he was fantastically attracted to me. She was very cruel to me at times. For example, once she turned up at my flat and gave me a lecture in front of a friend of hers . . . she hurled abuse at me in front of this friend for nearly an hour, refusing to get out of the flat because she said it belonged to her husband.'

Trying to remain polite in such a tense situation is almost impossible. One mistress felt completely at the mercy of the wife, and felt she had to answer the phone even though she knew it would cause further anguish.

'His wife used to ring me up all the time, initially just to abuse him. But when that failed to destroy our relation-

100

ship, she started to tell lies. The first time I believed her. She told me he had come around after a business trip with all his gear and promised to move back home again, when in fact she hadn't set eyes on him. When he finally moved in with me (or I thought it was finally) she would ring up every night, at about midnight, and scream and cry and blackmail him, telling him she was going to take tranquillizers to kill herself and so forth.'

In one instance the reverse happened. The mistress and wife had got together and not only discovered they had a lot in common but also that they liked each other enormously; their exchanges were therefore supportive rather than recriminatory. However, this was an exceptional case.

The mistress is often condemned on all sides – by her demanding lover, wives, society and by herself. And the ultimate paradox of her invidious situation is that, in a society where a woman's status is measured mainly by her ability to attract and snare a man, the mistress is condemned for being so successful.

A wife, because of her relationship with her husband, has financial security, social acceptability and status and general approval, while the mistress, because of her relationship with the same man, has none of these vicariously-gained advantages. She is robbed of dignity and position because she is a free woman having a relationship with an 'unfree' man.

'Being a mistress is the worst of both worlds. It takes a certain sort of personality to always play a double role and not go round the bend. I'm sure this is why most people settle for what they've got in the end.'

10 The Mistress - The Marriage-Breaker

'I'm a very ordinary man who would have gone on being married for ever if I hadn't been so besotted with a woman. I'd been married thirteen years when I met her and I was completely knocked over. We saw each other constantly for seven months and when I realized how important she was to me I told my wife and asked for a divorce.

'But nothing happens as easily as that. It took a year for the situation to resolve itself. I felt so guilty about what I was doing to my wife and my children and about the responsibilities that I wanted to ease my conscience by trying to lessen the effect of my decision to leave. We'd had a good marriage till that point.

'My to-ing and fro-ing between my wife and my mistress caused distress to my mistress as well. She was convinced the marriage was terrible and I think this salved her conscience. Katharine Whitehorn once began an article on advice to second wives with the line "Rule 1: Never assume that the first wife was a bitch." I think that's absolutely right. My mistress couldn't believe it.

'My wife was understandably resentful about my leaving her for another woman. She had reason to be upset, our children then were twelve and eight, the worst possible ages for their parents to break up. But I had no idea that her bitterness would make her so revengeful – she used the children as a form of blackmail and even now, eight years later, my children haven't accepted my mistress. My wife has constantly called her "the woman who took Daddy away from Mummy".

'I was leading a fairly typical upper-middle-class life

before this happened, and there I was at the age of forty throwing it all over to go and live in a flat in the middle of London. It was a hell of a break. I think most men are like me – they wouldn't leave home until there were welcoming arms waiting. I know of only one man who left his marriage without having another woman waiting in the wings.

'I'm sure very few men leave home because of the mistress though. It's much easier to continue the status quo, perhaps having a mistress on the side. Usually men can put up with even the worst of marriages because they can survive by sublimating themselves in work or outside interests. The pattern a man builds up is comfortable, secure. He's not sure what he might get himself into if he broke up the marriage. At least by keeping the marriage going he has some control over tomorrow.

'I wasn't looking for a long-term affair when I met the woman who became my mistress. I saw it as temporary, but after three months I realized I was passionately in love, in a way I'd never been before. I was obsessed by her, and that's the only reason why my marriage broke up. I couldn't in all honesty continue a relationship with my wife knowing that I felt so much for another woman. It would have been too messy and complicated to keep a secret affair going. I'm not the sort of person who lies and dissembles with ease.

'With the wisdom of hindsight it's awfully difficult to say whether I did the right thing. Had I known the agony and pain of it beforehand I might not have done it. I just didn't know what I was letting myself in for.

'I still love my mistress but I am cynical about this true love that writers and others are always holding up as the pinnacle of experience between a man and a woman. I don't think there is such a thing. When my marriage broke up and I left I was definitely going to marry my mistress. We just had to wait till the divorce came through. It took six years before my wife got herself into a frame of mind where she could actually go into a court about a divorce. In that time of waiting my mistress became very bitter. In fact the whole period of disentanglement caused scars that haven't healed. She even today seethes with jealousy when I mention my wife or arrange to meet her and the children.

'Our years together have been very hard because we inherited the baggage of a broken marriage. All the guilt and resentment were transferred from one relationship to the other. We should have faced up to them. But we didn't and they have eroded our relationship.

'Perhaps it was because I was so obsessed by her that I didn't realize the incompatibilities between us. Every so often a little red flag would wave in my mind and I'd feel uncertain, wary, but I ignored all these warnings. I pushed them into the back of my mind believing that love would help us overcome and iron out all these difficulties.

'Living together brought out all the basic incompatibilities. She's a career woman and we compete with one another. All sorts of jealousies and problems crop up from this. The differences between us made it impossible for us to live together and now we have separate flats. We still see a great deal of each other but between us is a sort of love–hate. We can only survive by living apart.

'My wife was the exact opposite of my mistress. She had never worked and she made being a wife and mother a career. She was very good in the domestic sense; she was really somewhat of a *hausfrau*. My mistress is completely independent and I can't say which of the two ways I like better. The problems with my mistress seem immense and I can't see what will happen to us eventually. But we're still in love. At least we seem to need one another.

'I don't know that we'll ever marry. What we imagined each other to be eight years ago has been proven false. I

104

don't think we've yet found in each other what we're looking for and if we had both faced up to those resentments instead of pushing them aside we might have had a happier relationship today. I couldn't have gone on being married to my wife – it wouldn't have been fair on her feeling the way I did about my mistress.'

Mistresses who cause a marriage to break down are comparatively rare. While the existence of a mistress and her subsequent discovery might be a catalyst to a marriage breakdown, she herself is not the reason for the failure. She is usually a symptom of an already established incompatibility.

A marriage guidance counsellor explains: 'The need for an ongoing external relationship occurs when a large part is missing from a marriage,' and this was certainly borne out in our sample. Of the thirty-five women we interviewed, only two played any part in a marriage breakdown, and in neither instance could her part be said to be decisive. The seeds of the marriage failure had been sown long before the mistresses had entered their lovers' lives.

The marriages of two men we interviewed had also broken down, but only one man – our case history – attributed it to his mistress. He was happily married till she came along, he insists, but so besotted with her that he abandoned marriage and family in pursuit of 'la grande passion'.

This brings up the question of what makes a 'good marriage' as opposed to a bad one. The husband in the case study had a most domestic wife who saw to his every need, who was a good mother to his children, who had never worked and was dependent on him financially and emotionally. In temperament they were suited – until he discovered he was capable of deeper emotion.

The rest of the men we interviewed described their relationships with their wives in a variety of ways ranging from non-existent to very good. But in six cases the men said their wives didn't boost their egos, didn't make them feel important or attractive. In nearly all cases sex with the wives was perfunctory – merely one of the expected roles of a husband. In most cases the men realized that they had changed considerably in their years of marriage and that their wives had not changed apace.

'I like my wife. She's a nice person but I don't love her in the sense of lusting after her. I'm not on the same wavelength as she is. Ten minutes of conversation and that's it – we have nothing in common. She's a good woman, a marvellous wife and mother, but she's just not my sort. There is a failure but I don't want to break up my marriage because of the children.'

The other man in our sample whose marriage broke up while he was involved with a mistress explained how he had been aware of a widening chasm in his marriage well before he began to get involved in an affair.

'For several years before I met my mistress I found myself drifting away from my wife. I became more and more attracted to other women and I flirted madly, at first I suppose because of the excitement of it, but after a while I began to realize that I was particularly attracted to women who were the opposite of my wife. Slowly, especially in my present affair, it dawned on me just how much I was depending on these other women to supply all those things I wasn't getting in my marriage. Only through them can I make my marriage survive.'

As we have discussed earlier, very few men, it would seem, are prepared to leave home without the reassuring, welcoming arms of another woman, which is a reason why mistresses can almost inadvertently find themselves acting as a catalyst in a breakdown.

'I doubt I would have left my wife if my mistress hadn't been there to go to. I'm basically a coward and I wouldn't have done anything about leaving. My mistress decided it for me.'

A mistress can find herself playing the role of a safety-net, giving a husband the moral support and strength to take the initial leap. But usually the mistress has no control over whether or not she will be called upon to play a part in the saga of a marriage break. With the rare exception of the 'bitter' mistress who rings her lover's wife, or an interfering outsider who feels 'duty bound' to inform about an affair, almost invariably the decision to tell or not to tell is left with the husband.

Precipitating a crisis will often do the job. A letter left casually in a pocket, a thoughtless remark that can only arouse suspicion – actions like this will get reaction. One husband told us how he'd planned for months beforehand so that the letter would be found at the right time. But while no others were as overt as this, most realized in retrospect that subconsciously they had wanted to be found out. Once they had deliberately provoked the crisis, they were forced to make a decision about leaving.

'After I'd told my wife about my mistress I felt better because now I didn't have to lie. The thing I hated most was that I was so successful at lying. It shook me more than anything that it was so easy. I often wished I'd been caught out so I wouldn't have had to go on lying.'

Almost all the mistresses in our sample realized they were unlikely to break up a marriage. This awareness obviously assisted some of them in rationalizing their behaviour and diminishing their conditioned feelings of guilt. When asked if they thought mistresses tended to break up marriages, eight were unsure, but the response of the other twenty-seven mistresses was immediate and categoric: 'No! I think if anything they tend to keep them together.' 'It's the other way round. Men don't take mistresses unless they've got a shaky marriage in the first place.' 'The only time a mistress breaks up a marriage is when the marriage is vulnerable. In other words, when it's rotten or dead.'

But this recognition didn't stop seven mistresses from wishing for or fantasizing about a miraculous, painless ending to their lovers' marriages. Several confessed to nurturing a secret wish that the wives of their lovers would suddenly die, run off with another man, or at any rate disappear from the scene.

But mistresses' dreams must stay in the privacy of their fantasy world. (To be a mistress it is necessary to be fairly realistic about the fact that a lover's marriage is unlikely to end.)

When the lover's marriage eventually does break down, confrontation will occur. The husband, wrenched from the comforts and habitual security of his family home, will not settle easily into a sparsely-furnished bachelor-girl flat.

'It's bloody miserable when you first separate, because the one who leaves has to find a new place to live. He's deprived of all his familiar things and his familiar haunts. Then of course, being the initiator of the separation, he bears this load of hostility from other people. All our friends clustered around my wife and I suddenly stopped being invited out. Then there's the financial hardship of it. I had nothing. The only thing I took was my stereo set and so I had to get furniture and crockery and all that sort

of thing. From a very comfortable standard of living I was like a bloody penniless student. I had one knife and one fork and one spoon. The main reason I survived was because of this other woman. She helped me through this critical period, which was an enormous help. It was a bloody miserable time, I must say.'

Apart from the physical discomforts, an ex-husband carries with him all the left-overs of his marriage — the unresolved feelings of guilt, doubt, resentment and uncertainty. His metaphorical little black bag will contain all the problems of his marriage and these will be an added weight, another strain, on their relationship.

In other words, if a mistress is involved in a marriage breakdown she will go through all the agony and heartache of the breakdown, almost as much as the husband and wife. Inescapably her relationship with her lover will be profoundly affected.

While many men may dream of quietly and abruptly disappearing with their mistresses, free from all responsibilities and commitments, few are able to translate these dreams into reality. In fact, when the crunch comes and the husband is confronted with the emotional crisis of the breakdown, his courage and determination often dramatically evaporate. Faced by the anguished, embittered cries of his resentful wife and the stricken faces of his confused children, many men are paralysed into indecision and uncertainty. Is it worth all the pain? Can I endure all this guilt? Some men run for cover at this stage.

'He stayed for three months because he felt he had to make a stand, but he knew all along he'd go back to his wife and family. He couldn't bear the thought that his daughter, who he really did love, would turn against him. We saw each other only to talk in that time. Our affair was over.'

The only relationship we found which had survived the breakdown and evolved into a 'permanent' affair – our case history – still bears the scars of the anguished transition. The consummation of his 'grande passion' never came about, and he and his mistress have reverted to a situation where they live separate lives in separate flats, seeing one another only as often as they did when they were lovers enjoying the intensity and excitement of an illicit affair.

The moral of this would seem to be: if a mistress is looking for a husband, she would be wise not to chose a married man, for the chances of a man actually leaving his marriage because of an affair are slim. It takes more than a mistress to break up a marriage. And the chances of a mistress and lover getting married after the break are even slimmer.

11 The Mistress - The Marriage-Maker

'At the beginning of our relationship I was young enough to think I had been the cause of his marriage break-up. But when the crisis was over and he went back to his wife, the feelings we had for each other for the next seven years kept his marriage going.

'I was twenty-five when I met him. We worked together and we both realized that there was an enormous attraction. I was engaged at the time but it wasn't till after I was married that the affair started. I wanted to be equal, you see; he was married, so I had to be married too. I had no intention of attacking or trying to oust his wife and the two children.

'My husband and I only saw each other at weekends because he was away at university, and my lover's family lived far enough outside the city for him to be able to find reasons why he couldn't get back at night. We had plenty of freedom. At first we stayed in hotels, then we rented a flat which he wouldn't let me pay for. It was separate from both our ways of life, a place for our meetings. We were in love and we knew we had to maintain double lives to stay in love.

'Then without consulting me he told his wife he wanted to leave her. I was really furious with him. I knew I wasn't stealing from her and it seemed to me essential that he was dishonest with her to save her suffering. But no. He went and told her. I was angry because he should have had more foresight. He deserved the way his wife reacted. Her pride was hurt. She was determined to get her revenge and the best way was through the children because my lover was a devoted father. She told one

111

of the twins, the one he was particularly attracted to, that Daddy didn't love him any more. He started having nightmares and everyone was very worried about him. He saw this son as a replica of himself and when he responded the way he did, he felt under attack.

'My lover felt he had to do what he said he'd do and he left home, but after three months he went back. I'd stopped seeing him from the moment he told his wife. I decided to leave my job and go and work nearer to my husband. I had the best intentions of making our marriage work but I couldn't get my lover out of my mind. I was having hallucinations, seeing him everywhere. I would rush up to someone I thought was him, but the face would turn into a stranger's.

'At this point we made contact again, and for eighteen months we met once, twice a month. During this time we realized just how deep our relationship was. Our most important realization was that there were two strands to both our lives and it would be a terrible mistake to get them intertwined.

'When my father learnt about the affair, I remember him saying: "Don't hurt other people and keep your tongue in your head." I thought he was being cynical, but he was right . . . it is important not to hurt other people.

'It was an enlightening and enlarging experience knowing my lover. I'd been to a school for young ladies and my background was very narrow. It was like coming out of a tunnel into the light. And I learnt something about myself I hadn't known before – what turns me on most about a man is kindness. My lover was not only kind to me but he was also kind to his wife and children after that first bad error.

'Actually it was his kindness that gave me the worst hurt in those seven years. It was the one time he was unfaithful – with a tart he'd given a lift to after they'd left the same pub. She'd invited him in and he felt it good manners to accept. He made love to her just as he did to his wife—because it was good manners to. I was upset because I felt he didn't owe the tart anything. But he used sex as a language. He used to say, "If it were demanded of me socially, I would make love to a gorilla."

'Our double lives continued even more scrupulously. I think being a mistress is the worst of both worlds. It takes a certain type of personality to always play a double role and not go round the bend. I'm sure this is why most people settle in the end for what they've got, rather than pursue something that only gives joy occasionally. But I know one thing – if we ever had married it would have been essential for us both to have been faithful because we both knew just how capable we were at lying. Having to continually hide things was a shattering experience.

'Everything in our sexual relationship was acceptable to me. I had never had an orgasm before I knew him – that was the thing that really came as a shock to me. I thought of us as a mystic union and I used to get annoyed when after we'd made love he'd have a cigarette. It was almost like smoking in church. It put our love on a mundane, everyday level.

'When we eventually started to break up I wanted him to make love to me more often because this brought us closer together mentally. By this time my own marriage had finished but the reasons for that went back to long before the marriage, to two children being unable to grow up. We had nothing in common and it took marriage to prove it to us.

'Then I met a man who asked me to live with him. I was tired of living life alone, of only seeing my lover when he could get away from his responsibilities. This man needed me, he made me feel wanted. He was very kind to me and I realized I wanted to let this man give to me. I felt I was the one who was always giving, first to my

113

husband who wanted a mother, then to my lover who was using me as a means of keeping his marriage together. I liked the change.

'I went to live with him and for the first few months I went on seeing my lover, though we both knew our relationship couldn't last much longer. We'd changed jobs so we weren't in competition in the same office. We'd both proved we were equal so who could dominate who didn't matter. We just ran out of steam. But it took a long time to end. We kept avoiding the decision because sex was good to the end. When it came I was really quite emotionally affected. I never thought I would be, but I felt sad that this passion would no longer be in my life.

'Just before we broke up he gave me a fur coat. It was a joke, a thing to do with mistresses. He said he wanted to make love to me while I was wearing it. And of course we did. When we split up I put the coat in my wardrobe and it was several years before the emotion connected with it had died enough for me to wear it.

'I was very angry when I heard a year after we'd broken up that he was in the divorce courts. His wife got the divorce and it wasn't on grounds of adultery. There was no other woman involved, the marriage just came to an end. I think the relationship I had with him kept the marriage going for all those years. He was a better husband and father as a result. He went home happy, he had better understanding of others' feelings. I can only imagine what he must have been like in that last year without a relationship to sustain him. He needed more than a wife and family and as he was a selfish man he must have made his feelings known. If he'd started another deep relationship, his marriage might still be going today.'

Mistresses do not, by themselves, break up marriages. The

mistress and the role she plays keep a man happy in a marriage which, until her entry into his life, he had found frustrating and unrewarding. The mistress in our case history is just one of the twelve women in our sample who felt that the relationships they'd formed with their lovers had been responsible for the continuation of their marriages.

Almost everyone can point a finger or cluck the tongue in the direction of some marriage they have heard of, or read about, which succumbed (so rumour has it) to the guile of a mistress. It is this conception of the dangerous, marriage-breaking mistress which holds the public's imagination.

Even in this day of the so-called guiltless marriage it would be hard to avoid hearing about the scandals that blow up around divorces where another woman is involved. If the mistress is named the excitable Sundays feel it is only fair on the readers that they should know what this woman looks like. Her lover, of course, probably won't be considered worth picturing. These reports give us a false view, and lead us to assume that this is the norm.

In fact it is only the tip of the adultery iceberg: the submerged nine-tenths give a better picture. If people knew just how many affairs there are under their very noses they would realize that so-called marriage-breakers, while grist to the scandal-mongers' mill, are rare and isolated mistresses, and are not characteristic of the majority at all.

Unknowingly a mistress usually finds herself playing the role of marriage-maker. 'It is highly probable that adultery maintains far more marriages than it destroys,' wrote Alex Comfort in *Sex in Society*, and our sample bears this out.

Thirty out of thirty-five mistresses we interviewed were manifestly playing a marriage-making role, though they varied greatly in their recognition of it. As stated, twelve saw very clearly that men who were getting satisfaction in extra-marital relationships returned to their wives happier, and presumably better, husbands.

'His wife was too busy with her own life and the children's to ask him very often how he was, did he have any problems etc. I was always there to listen, to boost him up when he felt down. He never left the flat without a smile on his face.'

The woman in our case history obviously masked and compensated for the deficiencies in her lover's marriage. She met his extra needs for seven years and when the relationship broke up, he was faced with the frustrations that caused him to seek an extra-marital relationship in the first place. When they reappeared his marriage broke up – and there was no third party involved.

Several mistresses realized that their liaisons with their lovers were either started or given impetus by a strain in the marriage.

'In seven years I have learnt little about the substance of the relationship he has with his wife. I think it's a good marriage but she's the stronger partner. She's in control. I think I turned up at some point of crisis. That's passed but I'm still around. Their relationship has changed but it's not been ruined.'

Pregnancy is a particular stress-point in marriage and three mistresses realized in retrospect that the intensity of their relationships with their lovers increased during these times. One mistress who felt used because of this took the opportunity to test the depth of her lover's feelings for her when a second pregnancy occurred.

'I wanted to see whether our affair had only started because he had time on his hands, so I bloody-mindedly refused to have sex with him till the child was born. Our feelings for each other survived.'

In six cases wives discovered that their husbands were involved in long-term affairs, but divorce did not occur. Again, in *Sex in Society* Alex Comfort provides the explanation: 'The wife who has a lover or the husband who has a mistress are probably not enjoying the simplest form of sexual relationship though they may be adopting the most feasible and desirable solution for their particular needs, and any complications involved are a measure of their difficulties. These difficulties may inevitably include some injury to feelings, but they need not include guilt, anger, and outraged social dignity, nor the need to make, at any cost, the appropriate social gesture.'

Two of the married mistresses in our sample had to reassess their own marriages as a result of their extra-marital affairs, but both came to the conclusion that they wanted their marriages to continue.

'The sexual and mental rapport in an affair can endanger a marriage because inevitably in the course of a marriage many aspects tend to break down. So there's a general reappraisal of your own marriage and a lot of inevitable heartache and emotional wrangling. But if you feel your marriage is meaningful enough despite all the areas of incompatibility, then the affair can act as a catalyst for feelings you've been aware of but have sublimated. It can also be the means of holding your marriage together. This is what happened to me.'

The second married mistress, one who fits our definition of a free agent, feels that her marriage has been strengthened by her attitude and discoveries.

'I'm a happier person and sexually a better partner to my husband. Before I'd had an affair, our bed-time life became terribly stolid and boring. Being with someone else and doing different things means I'm bringing some things home, so sex with my husband has become more interesting.'

This mistress was adamant that she would lie if necessary to prevent her lover's wife finding out about the relationship.

'Denying it will keep the marriage together which is the main thing as far as I'm concerned. She's such an inoffensive person and a good wife and mother, why should she be hurt because of my hobby?'

Several mistresses were very wary of the idea of breaking up a marriage simply because they didn't feel they could face the problems that would result, especially where children were involved.

'If it got to the stage where it was a case of ending the marriage I would finish with him. I love him so much that I wouldn't destroy him. His kids are very important to him. I would like to marry him and have a child by him, but I would have to break the marriage up and that I couldn't do.'

Two mistresses, both American, made conscious decisions about their lovers and their marriages. Neither one would ever bring up the subject of her lover leaving his wife. One explanation was valid for both:

'I kept thinking of what would happen to the children. I am a child of a broken marriage and I know how much it hurt me.'

Four mistresses in our sample would undoubtedly have been horrified to realize they were playing a marriage-making role. This was a long way from their intentions for secretly they were hoping to become second wives. By demonstrating that they are incomparably better partners, they hope their lovers will decide to abandon their deficient marriages and seek a permanent, more legal relationship with them. The relationships had been going for between three and five years.

These four were very proud of the way they were able to put aside their own problems and to listen to complaints about work and marriage. They enjoyed boosting the ego. In short, they allowed their men to sound off, to be self-centred. What they couldn't see was that the deficiency in their lovers' marriages was now non-existent – the mistresses themselves had provided the paper for the cracks. Having got everything that worries them off their minds, the men probably bounce back into the domestic humdrum without a backward glance.

A mistress of twelve years' duration summed it up:

'Basically mistressing is all about communicating verbally as well as sexually. Until he met me my lover had never really talked to a woman. I fulfilled a need in his life that his wife couldn't. As we both wanted a little bit of life that wasn't respectable, we were happy.'

12 The Mistress - The Search for a Father Figure

'Having an affair with my lover was like having an affair with the King, the Pope, Charlie Chaplin and my father. I looked up to him as some all-powerful being. It all happened ten years ago but even now I remember with clarity how I just couldn't stop myself getting involved with him. And at the same time I knew I was petrified of him.

'I was a neurotic, upright product of a Catholic upbringing ... and a virgin. At the start of our relationship I was totally and utterly dependent on him. I was just a baby and it took me about seven years to grow up. It never occurred to me that he was attracted to me and I couldn't understand why he pursued me for six months. On the first night he made love to me I fell madly in love with him.

'He told me about his marriage but I didn't worry about his wife at all because I never thought I was important enough to him. I saw our relationship as being permanent but not ending in marriage. At least, in the early stages I did. Later, when I was sick of the situation as it was, I wanted to get married. I hated having to cart clothes all over London, having to get up an hour earlier so that I could get back to my flat before going on to work, not being about to commit myself to any of my friends – for lunches or dinners – in case he should ring.

'For about eighteen months I saw quite a lot of him. Then to try and get away from it all I went to Italy. He found me. He was very rich and he could afford to go wherever he wanted. Out of the blue he would ring and say, "Meet me in Strasbourg" or "Meet me in Paris". I was travelling all over the place to meet him. I decided to return to Britain and we started spending three or four week-nights together, then weekends.

'From a social point of view being a mistress brassed me off. He would never enter my world at all. I had my own flat and my own friends – I think he thought they were inferior and didn't want anything to do with them. I always had to go to his house. He'd left his wife by this time and I hated the house he lived in. I'd never try and change a thing. These all seem small things but they really worried me. I gradually became very neurotic – I had become unhappy with the affair because I was unhappy with myself.

'He was very generous. He gave me five years of psychiatric treatment. It was very good of him. He wouldn't try to help me himself but he would pay to help me. Otherwise he didn't want to know.

'He was constantly making me feel inadequate. I know I was difficult and very young but he did nothing to help my ego. He was extremely possessive of me and he would never accept that I had any other life outside the one I had with him. He just didn't care for what I was really like.

'I think he put me down as a woman. He knew how much I hated the stuffy business dinners he was always giving, yet he insisted that I be there. The people who went to those dinners really treated me badly, the women especially, and the disapproval they all felt for the relationship was obvious. Now I know of course that the way he treated me helped me grow up, but it was a very painful experience.

'He was unfaithful throughout the whole ten years. He was a very rich, powerful man and he picked up women like horses pick up horseflies. I was never concerned if a quick fuck was all that was involved, but twice he told me

E*

he'd found the woman he wanted to marry. That hurt – and the fact that he didn't marry either of them showed that he liked getting this jealous reaction from me.

'The women he took up with for some reason wanted to tell me about it; they either rang me or my friends, and there I was in the ludicrous situation of saying "there, there" to some stranger who was suffering because of my lover. I used to wonder whether he talked to them about me deliberately to see what would happen. Despite all this I respected him. I knew he was dishonest with his wife, with me, with his other women. Yet I respected him. I can't even explain why.

'My friends kept at me to end the affair. They thought he was bad for me and took every opportunity to tell me so. They never met him and I think they made him out to be really worse than he was, but after all, they were the ones who had to pick up the pieces when it got too much for me. I can understand why they tried to help.

'My relationship with him totally changed my life. I don't think he cared for me very much but he was better for me than any other man has ever been. He did the important things, like send me to a shrink when I needed it, and looked after me. He never thought I was good enough for him, certainly not good enough to be his wife.

'I did consider myself a mistress. By that I mean somebody who takes up with a married man but who is removed from his ordinary life, someone who participates in an intense relationship outside the real world. The two have separate lives, separate houses and separate worlds. I was like a simultaneous wife and those ten years of our involvement were as important and valid as any bad marriage.

'He wasn't generous with money but he improved as time passed. In the end he gave me quite a lot. In fact today he pays me £500 a year, what I call my alimony. I feel I deserve it after all the years I gave up to him, and because he took so much away from me.

'But I got other rewards from the relationship. He brought me up in effect. He was twenty years older than me and, as I said, he was like the Pope and my father rolled into one. The way he treated me forced me to find out about myself. I learnt a lot about how tough life can be. After my cloistered upbringing I needed to learn that.

'I'm sure he didn't get involved with me as a way of ending his marriage. The relationship we had wasn't a symptom of failure of his marriage so much as a symptom of failure in his personality. Not long after we broke up he married again.

'One of the reasons why he left his first wife was sex. At the start our sexual relationship was quite good, but after a while it was just as boring as anyone else's. All my friends think he "ruined" me because I've never had or wanted a permanent relationship since. But the various sexual experiences I've had with other men – married men – have proved to me one thing. He was a lousy lover. A god he might have been, but he was a lousy lover.'

Running through the majority of the mistresses' comments about their lovers was evidence of a search for a father figure. Not one had become involved with a man of her own age and the age differences ranged from five to twenty-five years. In all but one case, the man was doing a more responsible job and had a different degree of power through it.

'My three lovers have all been very similar. They were all ten years older than me, extraordinarily successful, self-confident and intelligent – I admired and respected them all, both as people and for the positions they were

123

in. I realize in retrospect that they all resembled my father to an uncanny degree. He was a very strong man and he had a great influence over me.'

Not all the mistresses we interviewed were as explicit as this, nor did all of them mention their fathers, but when describing their lovers they constantly stressed the respect and admiration they had for them, the recognition they had for their power and influence.

Particularly if the woman herself was independent, self-confident and somewhat aggressive, she made a point of mentioning that it was hard for her to find someone she could 'look up to in the callow youths of my own age' (as one mistress put it).

Each appeared to be seeking a partner who would dominate her, or at least a partner she couldn't dominate. Subconsciously the mistress seems to need to be dependent on a man, hence the attraction to men who are older, more experienced – and married.

'After my first affair I vowed I would never go out with a married man again. Then I met this guy through a friend at work. I found him extremely physically attractive and good to talk to as well. He was confident and positive and I liked that.'

Kindness and understanding came high on the list of sought-after or appreciated qualities. This was especially the case with women who wanted to be looked after and taken care of, again in what was manifestly a paternal sort of way.

'He managed his life with ease. He never seemed bothered by anything that went wrong – the meal not being ready on time, me arriving late, that sort of thing. When I was feeling low he'd cuddle me and soothe me

down. *He always seemed to know exactly what I was feeling. I knew that any decision he made would be the right one and I left all the organization of the affair to him.'*

In some cases the mistresses allowed themselves to be dominated for a different reason, to help them develop, to grow up as did the woman in our case history. The domination implies mistreatment, harsh exchanges, hurt — but this is acceptable for a period.

'He was an absolute bastard but he taught me so much. I think I looked on him as my mother looked on her husband. He too was a bastard, but he transformed her from a naïve girl to a talented woman. I thought my lover would do the same for me. I was totally miserable for the whole affair – and yet in a way it was what I wanted.'

This mistress had left home at an early age because of the dominant father. Now at the age of twenty-six, with the help of her two disastrous affairs, she is a much stronger, more rounded person. She rose above the dominance and learnt from it.

Another mistress of similar age welcomed the influence of her older married lover because he fulfilled a need in her.

'The relationship is good in that it's completely honest and open. There's a lot of kindness in it. He's ve~ siderate and he's been a stabilizing in~ needed that. Now I'm not sure I become more independent.'

The mistress whose lover v had had a strong attachment went to university. Her lover relationship as a background to other relationships'. In the early, intense part of the affair, the involvement cut her off entirely from other men, but now two years later it has given her a sort of freedom.

'I can't help comparing other men with him because he's very good – especially sexually. He's an important emotional support. The fact that he's older and has strength in areas that I haven't means he can push me in areas I don't believe in myself. He represents security to me.'

One mistress whose father had left her mother a week after she was born, found herself seeking him in every man. From her mother's description she had a picture in her mind's eye of the type of man he was, and if any man measured up to it she responded sexually to him. Involved now in her second long-standing affair, she is aware of the insecure base of the relationship.

'I feel I am trying to prove that if I had been my mother my father would not have left. I don't want to believe he left because of me – I have to believe he went away because of something my mother did. My lover tries very hard to understand this but it places a large burden on our relationship. I sometimes feel I'll never find happiness until I actually find my father.'

One woman, who at twenty-nine is adamant that she is more mistress material than marriage material, has tried to analyse the reason why. She feels it has something to do with the fact that as a child of divorced parents she ved with her mother from the age of two to nineteen.

father married the woman who was his mistress
moved so far away from where we lived that I

never saw him during all the years I was growing up. He's only known me as an adult. He realizes he has failed me because a girl-child needs a father to help her identify in a relationship. I never can do that. I've had two affairs now, both lasting three years. I don't want them to last any longer.'

Does it all stem from the psychological theory that all little girls want to marry their father? Are mistresses more prone to this idea than other girls in love? One of the mistresses we met could almost be in a parent–daughter arrangement because she's in constant contact with the wife as well as lover to the husband.

'I meet and discuss the relationship with her. Our meetings are productive because we both feel that the person in the wrong is him. He's not mature enough to make decisions. I understand the reality of the marriage because she's getting on and doesn't think there'll be anybody else for her. I regretted having got involved but it was too late. Perhaps I should say I allowed myself the luxury of regretting having got involved, but I didn't mean it since I allowed myself to continue in it.'

Knowing both the husband and wife made this mistress aware of her youthfulness, of her power to appeal to them both. She felt she gave equal understanding – she has become the ideal daughter in fact. Her own relations with her father were very good, though they were less so with her mother.

At the start of the relationship she felt she had found Mr Right. Meeting the wife proved it to her. Just as she had tried to come between her parents, she is succeeding in coming between her lover and his wife.

This is certainly an unusual case because very few of the mistresses got to know the wives at all. However, the majority were certainly seeking the strong know-it-all men, the powerful figures they remembered from their childhood. They see them as potential husbands, not realizing the problems that would result if their dreams came true.

Because of the uncertainty of the relationship she has with her lover, a mistress can find herself re-creating that stage of adolescence where she becomes aware of having to deserve love. She plays out the game which she has learnt from her father – fulfil my expectations and I will love you. This fatherly love, unlike the unconditional motherly love, relies on being loved because of one's merits. In the mistress, as in the child, it causes doubts, fears: if I do not please him perhaps love will disappear.

Fearing loss of his love, she feels she has to work hard to keep it. She looks to his authority and guidance and doesn't challenge his treatment of her because she believes that love can be lost if she does not do what is expected.

The mistress in our case history felt she had to win, had to be deserving of her lover's love. This essential immaturity resulted in neurosis which only a psychiatrist could do anything about. As a child she had had a strong attachment to her father and she transferred her need for his protection to her lover who, unfortunately for her, was undisciplined in his own life and very demanding of her. He made her feel inadequate rather than encouraging in her a sense of competence; he deflated her ego and wanted her in his life only on his terms.

Understandably, the major result of 'deserved' love is bitterness, a feeling of not being loved for yourself, but only because you please. The conclusion can be only that you have not been loved at all, but used. Therein lies the tragedy of many mistresses today.

13 The Mistress - The Symbol of the Failure of Monogamy

THE MISTRESS

'At first it was just one-night stands with us. I'd met him when we both worked on the same exhibition for my firm. My reaction to him was totally physical. I hadn't thought he was aware of me but after the exhibition he invited me to have a meal. By the end of it I'd had a lot to drink and I knew that I fancied him. We went to his flat and slept together.

'It developed from that, really. We saw each other two nights, then three nights, then four nights a week and eventually decided to get a flat together. I knew right from that first night that he was married, that he went to his home in the country every weekend. He felt very responsible about his children and I believed in and admired him for being so concerned about them. They are very young and they need him. I realized early that he needs them too.

'I know very little about his wife. Of course, she comes up in conversation, but this doesn't really give me any clue of what she is like as a person. He is very good friends with her and I accept her existence completely. I don't know what he tells her – she knows, I think, that he has someone, but not who he has. We've been together two years now so she must suspect something. I think that she just accepts that if his job is going to keep him away from her all week, he will need someone else. It wouldn't worry me if I met her or never met her and I've never given a thought to what would happen if she found out that the relationship was more than fleeting.

'I'm happy the way we are. I have no reason to resent anything because my lover and I have a good time together. He's not the least bit possessive but sometimes I have small jealousies – mainly to do with his attraction for women. But I never let my jealousy show. I realize it's not important. I always know that at the end of the night we'll go back to our little flat together.

'I am faithful to him but only for the reason that I haven't found anyone better I want to go to bed with. But even if I went to bed with someone else it wouldn't be a problem. It wouldn't affect our relationship because there's more to it than the physical side.

'He's been very good for me – but dreadful for my figure. He loves to cook. I don't know that it is a good idea to get involved with a man who likes to cook, to experiment; my clothes never fit me and as we are on a tight budget I can rarely buy any more. But then again he loves to sew as well as cook, so he makes all my clothes. I've got a perfect life. As he's now trying to build up his own business he works from the flat so he keeps that tidy. I go out to work but the money I earn is for us to share.

'I never think whether he has the best of both worlds. I think *I* have the best of both worlds. I have my free time whereas he is either with me or with his wife and family. As for him using me, well I think I use him – sexually at least! Our sex life is good. As I had only slept with one man before him, the whole sex bit is an experiment for me.

'At first my parents were against me living with him. My mother was specially wary because he is married. I wanted them to meet him but I wouldn't go unless they agreed that I be allowed to sleep with him at their house. It took them a while but they eventually accepted this and the visit was a great success. His cooking did it – they've never eaten so well. When we had to leave one flat to find another, we went to stay with them for two weeks and that won them over completely. My friends now accept the situation as well. They like to see him as well as me, but I like to keep my friends for the weekends when he's not here.

'I rather like the idea of being called a mistress. It's certainly better than being called a girlfriend, but it has no special meaning for me. When people we don't know well find out about the situation they think first of the wronged wife and assume that I must be a brazen hussy. After a while they get to understand that we are really quite ordinary people – not too depraved or different from them. But there are still problems involved in living with someone you're not married to. For example, to get our flat we had to pretend to the landlord that we are married.

'I am in love with this guy but I don't want to marry him. I am not the type who needs such security. His marriage was a good one at the start, I think – but I don't think it is good, bad or anything else at the moment. If anything did go wrong to upset the arrangement we have now, I certainly would not assume that I would become a second wife. Even if I had a child, which I won't because I'm on the pill, this wouldn't change my attitude. We have a great thing going for us. It could last ten months or ten years. But who wants to look that far ahead anyway?'

THE LOVER

'At twenty I was part of that society syndrome that led to marriage. In our little country circle she was the best of the lot and everyone envied me for getting her. She was beautiful and quite a happy person. We had the same friends, the same interests, and as everyone expected us to get married we did. I thought I was in love with her, that it would be fun to put together a house with her.

'By nature I am attracted to women. I think my first affair occurred about two years after marriage. Don't ask me to count how many I've had in the thirteen years since. My wife knew I slept around. I never told her, she worked it out for herself. The sex between us became a boring routine, something expected, something to be done.

'On the estate where we bought our house there are many blokes around twenty-five to thirty who put their slippered feet on the mantelpiece and with pipe in hand settle down to watch telly every night. That's never been what I would call happiness. I was never like them, not even in the early years of marriage.

'I don't know that I'm against marriage but I feel people shouldn't marry as young as we did. We were just in our early twenties. I feel sad that I wasn't more sensible then, that I didn't know better.

'But how could I? No young person listens to views on non-marriage and accepts them.

'I now have what you'd call a friendly marriage. My wife accepts that there must be someone else but I know she wouldn't want to know who it is. I don't like lying so I tell untruths – but only to protect her against her feelings. I wouldn't dream of telling her that I have this lovely chick up in London that I fuck every night.

'I have two lives but they go together well. I go home at weekends because of the children. I think they need me – and I need them.

'I know I'm an egotist. I think it's marvellous that my mistress thinks I'm attractive and tells me so. Before I met her I was having an affair a week – dreadful really, but great fun. Since we've got together I don't have affairs. I still meet women I'd like to fuck but the whole thing would take too much effort to organize.

'I don't think of my lover as my mistress. I don't know what a mistress is. It's an unfortunate term because its connotation seems to put her a slot lower than I would. She is my lover and I am hers – we are equal. Perhaps if I think of her as my mistress, she can think of me as my mister-ess . . . it's a thought. I wonder why there wasn't an equivalent term for men?

'If I could find someone rich enough I'd be a mistress. I can cook, clean, sew, keep a house straight. If there were a pretty powerful lady around who needed someone like me, I'd do it.

'I realized a long time ago that I'm the major threat to my marriage. My lover doesn't really come into it. If it wasn't her it would be someone else. I think the man is better off. He takes part in the world, is able to mature and change while the woman at home can only measure herself against other housewives. The man can go on and be whatever he wants to be and when he's successful he must feel that his wife lacks the qualities he needs in a consort. I just grew out of my marriage and we have become independent of each other.

'Could I have done more to encourage her to change, to try and keep up with me? I don't think so. I think I tried through the years but it's only lately that she's starting to think of herself, not just as a wife and mother. She's starting to realize that I might not come back one day and she'd better be prepared. She's doing some sort of part-time training so that she'll be qualified for a job if the present situation changes.

'I don't know whether my father had a mistress. I suspect he did. My parents were divorced and I remember my mother once saying to my wife, "he's just like his father." Perhaps I inherited my interest in women from him.'

'For a long time I have kept up the pretence that I don't know about his relationship. He's always been the sort to have affairs and it was a very painful discovery to make at the start of our marriage. I was especially upset when the first child was born and my hormonal problems weren't helped by knowing that he was in bed somewhere with another woman.

'I'll say this for him – when he realized just how much I had needed him he was unhappy because he knew he had failed me. But he's faithful to me and the kids in a way I admire. We are very good friends, and how many wives and husbands can say that? I think I value this more than "love" because friendship entails affection and respect and these to me are the most important feelings.

'I never took any of his affairs very seriously but when this one started it felt it was different from the others. He started coming home less and less and by the end of six months we'd fallen into the pattern of him coming home only at weekends. I got used to acting on my own, making decisions, organizing the family. To my surprise I found I rather liked not having to rely on someone else. Being able to act unilaterally helped me build up my confidence. At first he was a bit taken aback the way things ran so smoothly without him. But I never tried to break down his feelings for the children, or theirs for him. He became a sort of welcome uncle who appeared at weekends.

'He's never been stingy with money so this has given me freedom too. I can afford a baby sitter and can go out at night. I have several girlfriends and we go out to the pub or to the pictures. I've even joined a night class to learn a language. It was interesting trying to decide what I wanted to study. If the opportunity had been given me in the early part of the marriage I'd have chosen something practical like upholstery or dressmaking so that I could be better at being a wife. Now I am interested in being a better person, to find outlets that make me happy. The local university has started a new course to train people for social work and I've done one term there. I was nothing more than a shorthand typist before marriage and I keep thinking that if I have children to support I'll need something better. I have to learn to be completely independent.

'Strangely enough the person I have to thank most for showing that this capacity was in me is my husband. We didn't know each other when we got married. We were children with children and there was a lot of changing to be done before we found our personalities and realized our wants.

'I went right off the idea of sex after the kids were born but now that my confidence is coming back I'm getting more interested in sex. My husband and I have sex still, but only about twice a month. For me to reject him would make him think that I know about his other life. As it's going so well for all of us now, I wouldn't want to be the one to change it.

'I have met several men in the last few years but I'm not looking for a long-term affair. I'm too busy getting myself together. But I know that I look at men with a different eye now . . . one of the men at the French classes really turns me on. I keep wondering what it would be like to be in bed with him.

'Only one of my friends knows the situation. For the others we are living the way we do because my husband's work requires that he be away. We still have parties at the weekends as a married couple and we go to other parties as a married couple. I never get invited alone when he's away because wives around here aren't invited alone. I wish people would change that attitude. I like going out by myself, not as one half of a couple. I don't want my neighbours to start gossiping about me. I think the pretence we live with is worth it. It gives me time and that's something I need a lot of.

'Sometimes I wonder what my husband's woman is like. He's always happy at weekends so they must get on well together. I don't want to meet her – while I don't know her I can't feel anything about her. I certainly don't hate or blame her. If she were trying to bring the marriage to an end, to take my place, I think my husband would start showing signs of wear and tear. He likes his children and he likes me – I don't think he could discard us without a great deal of anguish. I'll just have to watch for signs. In the meantime I'll be concentrating on becoming as independent as I can so that I won't be shattered when he asks for a divorce. Even if he did marry again he'd still want his bit on the side. I wonder if she realizes that?'

Every modern mistress is a living, breathing symbol of the failings of monogamy. She holds up, in effect, a mirror to monogamy and exposes the hypocrisies and deceits that are present today.

We spare ourselves the discomfort of the mistress's gaze and escape the insistence of her message only by excluding her from direct vision. She becomes the scapegoat.

We project our deepest fears and fantasies on to her. But, at the same time, by ignoring her and confining her activities to the fringes of society we ensure that while she may be a threat to individual marriages, she will not be a threat to the institution of marriage.

We ensure that she, like the prostitute, is not only the victim of monogamy but its perpetuator as well. If by decree she were to disappear, monogamous marriage would probably collapse.

A mistress exposes several of the fallacies on which

monogamy is based. One of the greatest of them is the notion that for love to survive it must be enchained in a legal, contractual framework.

Yet love – as every form of propaganda portrays to us – is a spontaneous, irrational, uncontrollable passion. From advertisements, posters, literature and folk-lore we have been taught to expect that falling in love always verges on the abnormal and is always accompanied by blindness to reality, compulsiveness and physical weakness.

Although Erich Fromm argues in *The Art of Loving* that the character of this sort of popularized love is illusory and should more properly be called infatuation, it is nevertheless the 'love' we are conditioned to yearn for and expect.

The attempt to legalize and contain this essentially irrational love in a life-time contract – marriage – would work satisfactorily only if it were true that love for the majority of the population occurred only once in every life and endured for a lifetime. Given that the reverse is true it is scarcely surprising that so many of us are frustrated, tormented and for ever groping to find this supposedly devastating, all-embracing, once-in-a-life-time love.

The married couple today, having witnessed the fading of their infatuation, are virtually compelled by the strength of the 'love' propaganda to continue searching either consciously or sub-consciously for this idealized condition.

But whereas the single person is condoned and rewarded for the irrational behaviour commonly thought to characterize 'falling in love', the married person is condemned for precisely the same behaviour.

Just as the black man or woman is made to feel that to love another with a different-coloured skin is a criminal act, so the mistress and the married man are made to feel that their irrational, spontaneous, apparently genuine feelings of love constitute a crime. In fact, what is exposed each time another affair is publicly discovered is the contradiction between the legal, rational character of marriage and the spontaneous, irrational character of love which we have been conditioned to regard as a prerequisite of marriage.

Right up until Victorian times the distinction between the legal character of marriage and the irrational condition of love was recognized and accepted. Marriage more often took place for reasons of convenience – property, inheritance, dowries, for example – than for the reason of love.

Today in the western world we have tried to erase and ignore the contradiction. The abundance of extra-marital affairs is but one example of how the attempt has failed. Another of the fallacies of contemporary marriage is that one person will be able to satisfy all the needs of his and her partner. Not only, so the myth goes, will they love each other passionately till death them do part, but they will also continually and absolutely satisfy one another's every need.

In her book *The Female Woman* Arianna Stassinopoulis writes: 'Demosthenes said of the Athenian woman, "We have hetaeras for the pleasures of the spirit, concubines for sensual pleasures and wives to give us sons." Modern woman is expected to be all three to her husband – there is no doubt that the conception of the man-woman relationship in marriage has never been as complex and ambitious.'

In fact very few marriages have all the ingredients to satisfy a couple's mutual needs, but even so the expectation remains. It is this which accentuates the dissatisfactions and frustrations, especially if the couple live in what is being called more and more a 'closed' marriage.

An 'open' marriage is based on recognition of the

importance of mutual growth. Aware that one person cannot possibly fulfil all needs, partners in an open marriage accept that both should attempt to satisfy many of their own needs outside marriage – through work and social activities. In doing this they feel they will free the marriage of many of its traditional role-playing burdens, and that they will be better able to satisfy each other within the marriage.

It is probable that in an open marriage a mistress would be less important and less necessary. There is no doubt that the existence of the mistress today is largely a result of the rigid separate development of husband and wife in the traditional marriage.

In the traditional marriage, wives are effectively isolated in their homes as sole child-rearers for ten to fifteen years. In this situation, deprived of external stimulus and unable to develop productively their potential, they grow apart from their husbands and fail to develop at their pace.

Eventually, finding his wife increasingly boring and unstimulating after her years of semi-exile bringing up his children, a husband may seek a more vital, equal, unpredictable partner – a mistress. She may well resemble his wife as she was when they were first married.

So long as wives undergo a transformation by marriage into mothers and housewives, are domestically oriented to the exclusion of all else, are living lives totally divorced from their working husbands, then so long will the mistress – and the hunt for her – continue to flourish.

For the fact remains that it is virtually impossible for a woman, harassed by the demands of children and housework, to live the schizophrenic existence of mistress, mother, wife and domestic servant which advertisers and advice columnists see as her role.

Columnist Marjorie Proops, in exhorting wives to adopt

mistress tactics, wrote: 'Inside every wife there's a mistress ready to reveal herself ... if only she had time, patience and imagination to let the wife in her take second place.

'The other woman is not necessarily particularly sexy – or even young. She just takes more trouble and pays great attention to the subtle details of being desirable.'

In fact, despite what Marjorie Proops says, when the wife attempts to combine those many roles one of them must suffer – and invariably it is the role of being mistress to her own husband.

From our case history we see very clearly how the marriage did not live up to the expectations of both the husband and wife. They married at the most typical age – twenty-one. They had an average middle-class family – two children. They followed the conventional pattern of marriage – they bought a house and she stayed in it to bring up the children, while he ventured forth to make his mark with his work.

In these moulds they grew apart rather than together, to the extent where both recognize now that they lead 'independent existences'. The mistress in this case is clearly a symptom of a failing in the conventional marriage – the impossibility of two people in such diverse roles being able to satisfy one another.

If we look at this couple closely it was the popularized version of love that brought them to marriage. This love, really infatuation, was the first thing to go with the reality of living together. Fortunately these two have managed to remain friends instead of being bitter about their failed expectations. The mistress, by her understanding of her lover's needs, has obviously encouraged the friendship.

This marriage is a living example of the situation described by Arianna Stassinopoulis in *The Female Woman*: 'When marriage is merely the state of not being

140

divorced and when most pleasures – sexual and mental – are sought outside it, it is hardly surprising that legally marriage failures are few.'

The very existence of the mistress shows that all is not well in the state of monogamy today.

14 The Mistress - Conclusions

The most significant discoveries we made about the modern mistress are :

Except in her potential influence over her lover, she bears very little resemblance to the fantasized lady of the past.

She is not necessarily glamorous, and almost never a 'femme fatale'.

There is no general way to describe her – some of the most unexpected, unattractive women are playing her role.

She often suffers as much as any wife in an unhappy marriage situation.

She often becomes almost a second wife, as dependent on her lover as is a legal wife.

She is often as guilt-ridden as her lover, and sees herself as society sees her: 'the guilty one'.

She is unlikely to break up a marriage. She is much more likely to keep a marriage together.

If she plays the catalyst in a marriage breakdown she is unlikely to become the second wife of her lover.

She is an outgrowth of a conventional closed marriage, and the parallel relationship she forms with her lover usually contains the elements that disappear from a marriage that was based on infatuation.

The modern mistress is a scapegoat for the failings of monogamy, but she is too conditioned to stand up and declare her right to love.